TOP 10 CAIRO & THE NILE

ANDREW HUMPHREYS

DK
EYEWITNESS TRAVEL

Left **Smoking sheesha** Centre **Ibn Tulun Mosque, Cairo** Right **Tomb of Nakht, Tombs of the Nobles**

DK

LONDON, NEW YORK,
MELBOURNE, MUNICH AND DELHI
www.dk.com

Printed and bound in China by
Leo Paper Products Ltd.

First American Edition, 2009
13 14 15 16 10 11 10 9 8 7 6 5 4 3 2 1

Published in the United States by
DK Publishing, 375 Hudson Street,
New York, New York 10014

Reprinted with revisions 2011, 2013

Published in the UK by Dorling Kindersley Limited.

A catalog record for this book is available from the Library of Congress.

ISSN 1479-344X
ISBN 978 0 75669 680 1

Within each Top 10 list in this book, no hierarchy of quality or popularity is implied. All 10 are, in the editor's opinion, of roughly equal merit.

MIX
Paper from responsible sources
FSC
www.fsc.org
FSC™ C018179

Contents

Cairo & the Nile's Top 10

The information in this DK Eyewitness Top 10 Travel Guide is checked regularly.

At the time of going to press there was major political upheaval in Cairo. Every effort has been made to ensure that this book is as up-to-date as possible, but due to the rapidly changing situation, some political information may have since altered. In addition, details such as telephone numbers, opening hours, prices, gallery hanging arrangements and travel information are liable to change. The publishers cannot accept responsibility for any consequences arising from the use of this book, nor for any material on third party websites, and cannot guarantee that any website address in this book will be a suitable source of travel information. We value the views and suggestions of our readers very highly. Please write to: Publisher, DK Eyewitness Travel Guides, Dorling Kindersley, 80 Strand, London WC2R 0RL, UK, or email: travelguides@dk.com.

Cover: Front – **4Corners:** Huber/Reinhard Schmid main; **DK Images:** Rough Guides/Eddie Gerald bl. Spine – **DK Images:** Eddie Gerald b. Back – **DK Images:** Eddie Gerald tc, tr; Jon Spaull tl.

Left **Temple of Philae** Centre **View of Islamic Cairo** Right **Luxor Temple**

Left **The Sphinx, Giza** Right **Felucca sailing on the Nile**

Key to abbreviations
Adm *admission charge*

CAIRO & THE NILE'S TOP 10

TOP 10 Cairo & the Nile's Highlights

The Nile is synonymous with Egypt. Almost the entire population of the country is crammed onto the narrow fertile plain fringing the river. It was so during the ancient Egyptian era, when the temples and cities of the pharaohs rarely strayed far from the life-sustaining area of the Nile's banks. Today, the best way to experience Egypt is to explore the Nile, from the awe-inspiring Pyramids on the outskirts of the capital of Cairo in the north, to the great temples in the far south of the country.

Egyptian Museum 1

This is one of the world's greatest museums, not least for the treasures in the Tutankhamun galleries, but for the exhibits from every period of ancient Egyptian history. It has been calculated that if a visitor were to spend just one minute at each item, it would take more than nine months to see everything *(see pp8–11)*.

2 The Pyramids of Giza

The only survivor of the Seven Wonders of the Ancient World, the Great Pyramid and its two companions are no less wondrous now than they were when they were built four and a half millennia ago *(see pp12–13)*.

Mosque of Al-Azhar 3

In addition to the monuments of the pharaohs, Egypt has an unrivalled wealth of historic Islamic architecture stretching back to the 7th century. The Mosque of Al-Azhar in Cairo is one of the jewels of this heritage *(see pp14–15)*.

4 Karnak

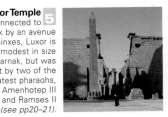

The mother of all ancient Egyptian temple complexes, Karnak was the powerbase of successive dynasties of pharaohs and the priesthood at the zenith of ancient Egypt's military and artistic might *(see pp16–19)*.

Luxor Temple 5

Connected to Karnak by an avenue of sphinxes, Luxor is more modest in size than Karnak, but was built by two of the greatest pharaohs, Amenhotep III and Ramses II *(see pp20–21)*.

Preceding pages **Colossus of Ramses II, Abu Simbel**

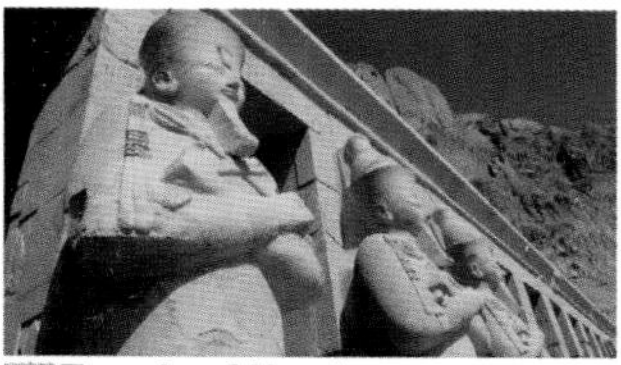

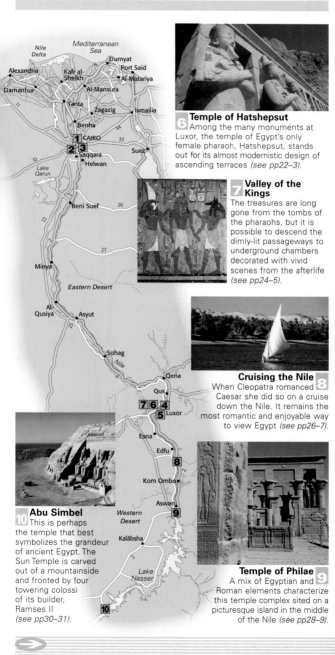

6 Temple of Hatshepsut

Among the many monuments at Luxor, the temple of Egypt's only female pharaoh, Hatshepsut, stands out for its almost modernistic design of ascending terraces *(see pp22–3)*.

7 Valley of the Kings

The treasures are long gone from the tombs of the pharaohs, but it is possible to descend the dimly-lit passageways to underground chambers decorated with vivid scenes from the afterlife *(see pp24–5)*.

Cruising the Nile 8

When Cleopatra romanced Caesar she did so on a cruise down the Nile. It remains the most romantic and enjoyable way to view Egypt *(see pp26–7)*.

10 Abu Simbel

This is perhaps the temple that best symbolizes the grandeur of ancient Egypt. The Sun Temple is carved out of a mountainside and fronted by four towering colossi of its builder, Ramses II *(see pp30–31)*.

Temple of Philae 9

A mix of Egyptian and Roman elements characterize this temple complex sited on a picturesque island in the middle of the Nile *(see pp28–9)*.

TOP 10 Egyptian Museum

All of ancient Egyptian history is here, from the earliest Pharaonic artefact ever discovered to treasures from the era of Cleopatra, the last in a dynastic sequence of divine kings and queens stretching over three millennia. It is said that the museum displays more than 120,000 items, with at least that many again stored away out of sight in the basement. The real crowd pleasers are the treasures from Tutankhamun's tomb, but there are many hundreds of other precious antiquities here of at least equal significance and beauty.

Central hall

The museum fills up fast, so arrive early to beat the worst of the crowds.

Cameras are not allowed inside the museum and must be left at a kiosk by the ticket office.

There is a café and a Mövenpick restaurant with indoor and outdoor seating as you exit the museum.

- *Map F3*
- *Midan Tahrir, Downtown, Cairo*
- *02 2578 2448*
- *Open 9am–6pm (last adm: 4:45pm)*
- *Adm £E60; Royal Mummy Room adm £E100*

Top 10 Features

1. The Museum Building
2. Auguste Mariette
3. Central Hall
4. Old Kingdom Galleries
5. New Kingdom Galleries
6. Amarna Room
7. Tutankhamun Galleries
8. The Royal Mummies
9. Animal Mummies
10. Ancient Egyptian Jewellery Rooms

1 The Museum Building

Egypt's first national museum of antiquities opened in 1863. It was rehoused in the current pink, purpose-built premises in 1902, which were designed in Neo-Classical style by French architect Marcel Dourgnon.

2 Auguste Mariette

The Egyptologist Mariette, who discovered the Serapeum at Saqqara *(see p40)*, was the founder of the first national museum of antiquities in Egypt. His sarcophagus rests in the garden in front of the Egyptian Museum *(below)*.

3 Central Hall

The museum is on two floors. On the lower floor galleries are arranged in chronological order clockwise around a central hall dedicated to statuary; this is also where the Narmer Palette is located *(see p10)*.

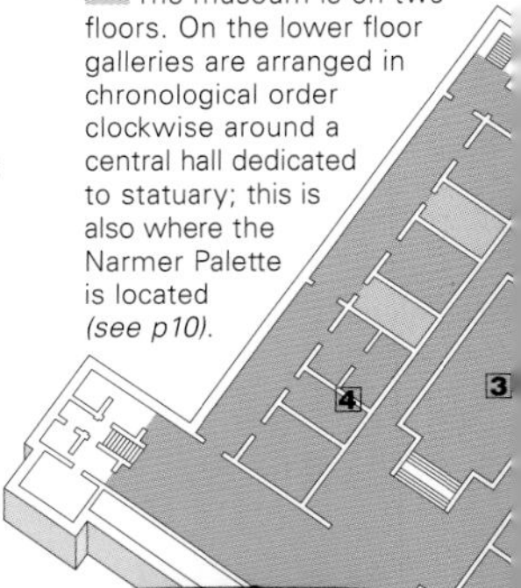

4 Old Kingdom Galleries

Immediately to the left of the entrance hall, these galleries contain artefacts from the era of the Pyramid builders. Particularly beautiful are three slate triads each depicting Menkaure, builder of the smallest of the Giza pyramids, flanked by two goddesses *(above)*.

For highlights of ancient Egyptian history **see pp34–5**

5 New Kingdom Galleries

This long gallery *(see exhibit left)* is devoted to the mightiest pharaohs, including Tuthmosis III, Amenhotep II and Ramses II, during whose rules Egypt expanded its borders south into what is now Sudan and north to the Euphrates.

6 Amarna Room

Room 3 contains pieces from Amarna, the short-lived capital of the "heretic king" Akhenaten *(see pp35 & 107)*. His daughter, Princess Meritaten, is characterized by an elongated face and full lips *(below)*.

Key

Ground floor

First floor

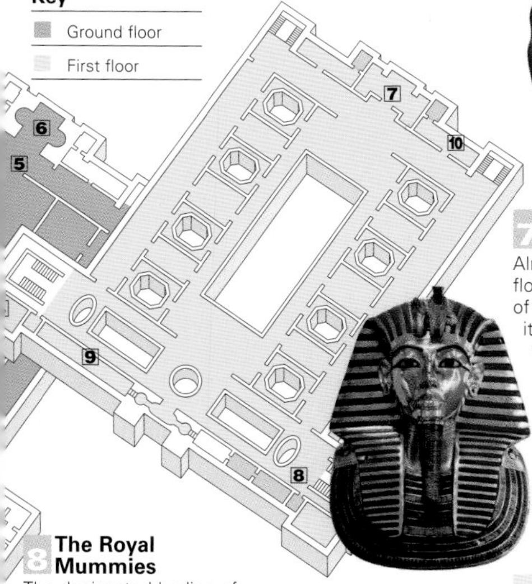

7 Tutankhamun Galleries

Almost half of the upper floor is devoted to some of the vast number of items excavated from the tomb of Egypt's famed boy-king *(left)*, which range from everyday items such as gaming sets and footstools to the giant gilded shrines and sarcophagi that fitted one inside the other like Russian dolls.

8 The Royal Mummies

The desiccated bodies of some of Egypt's mightiest rulers are displayed in two rooms on the upper floor of the museum. Of the eleven royals present, the most famous are Seti I and his son Ramses II, whose colossi adorn a great many monuments in Upper Egypt.

9 Animal Mummies

The ancient Egyptians mummified animals as well as people. This room on the upper floor of the museum is full of animal mummies, from cats, mice and fish to crocodiles, sacred to the god Sobek.

10 Ancient Egyptian Jewellery Rooms

These two rooms contain dazzling examples of royal jewellery from the New Kingdom period *(left)*. Many of these items were discovered in 1939 at Tanis, an ancient site in the Delta region.

Goodbye Tut

A new Grand Egyptian Museum is currently under construction close to the Pyramids. When finished, in 2015, it will house many of the items currently displayed at the existing Egyptian Museum, including the treasures of Tutankhamun. The museum on Tahrir Square will remain open to the public as a collection of highlights, offering an introduction to the ancient Egyptian world of the pharaohs.

Left **Statue of Ka-Aper** Centre **Detail of Tutankhamun's Lion Throne** Right **Detail of Narmer Palette**

Top 10 Egyptian Museum Masterpieces

Statues of Prince Rahotep and Nofret

1 Prince Rahotep and His Wife Nofret

Dominating Room 32 in the Old Kingdom Galleries are the twin life-sized, limestone statues of two seated royals of the 4th Dynasty. The pair lived four and a half millennia ago, but the statues' small details, such as the princess's real fringe poking out from under her wig and her elegant white dress, bring them back to life. The statues were discovered by the museum's founder, Mariette, at Meidum in 1871.

2 Narmer Palette

Dating from 3,000 BC, the Narmer Palette has been called the "first historical document in the world". It is a flat plate of greenish stone carved with designs that on one side show King Narmer (also known as Menes) wearing the White Crown of Upper Egypt and on the reverse, wearing the Red Crown of Lower Egypt. Historians interpret this to represent the unification of the two main tribes of Egypt under one ruler, making Narmer the founder of the 1st Dynasty and first king of all Egypt. This is when ancient Egypt started.

3 Statue of Ka-Aper

Egyptian art is not usually associated with realism, but so lifelike is this 5th-Dynasty wooden statue of the plump priest Ka-Aper that the workmen who discovered it at Saqqara in 1860 nicknamed him Sheikh al-Balad ("Head of the Village") because of the resemblance to their own headman. The eyes are extraordinary and are outlined in copper with whites of opaque quartz and rock crystals as pupils.

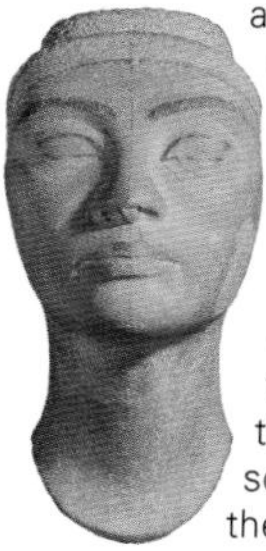

Sculpture of the head of Nefertiti

4 Head of Nefertiti

The best-known bust of Nefertiti is held by the Berlin Museum but the unpainted quartzite sculpture displayed in the Amarna Room of the Egyptian Museum is also a masterpiece. Although unfinished, it is a magnificent work and, in contrast to the almost grotesque depictions of her husband, Akhenaten, the queen is shown as a wholly human beauty.

5 Statuette of Khufu (Cheops)

Ironically, the only portrait of the builder of the famed Great Pyramid at Giza, the 4th-Dynasty king, Khufu, is a tiny ivory statuette just 7 cm (3 inches) high. It depicts the king sitting on his throne wearing a long robe and the crown of Lower Egypt and was found in a temple at Abydos in Middle Egypt. It now sits on its own in a cabinet in Room 37.

6 Tutankhamun's Lion Throne

There are around 1,700 items in the galleries devoted to the treasures of Tutankhamun. It is easy to be overwhelmed, but don't miss the Lion Throne. Its wooden frame is wrapped in sheets of gold and silver inlaid with semiprecious stones, faïence and coloured glass. On the back of the throne the young king sits under the rays of Aten (the sun) in a style derived from Amarna.

7 Tutankhamun's Death Mask

In a museum full of magnificence, the life-sized gold death mask of Tutankhamun remains the show stopper and the most famous example of ancient Egyptian craftmanship. It originally covered the head of the mummy and is an idealized portrait of the pharaoh. The gold of the headdress is interspersed with lapis lazuli and topped by a cobra that spits at the pharaoh's enemies.

8 Middle Kingdom Models

Several rooms on the west wing of the upper floor contain finely detailed models from the 11th Dynasty. These include peasants netting fish from a boat, cattle being driven past scribes recording their number, a platoons of soldiers of different ethnicities. Together they offer an invaluable insight into the daily life of the humble ancient Egyptian.

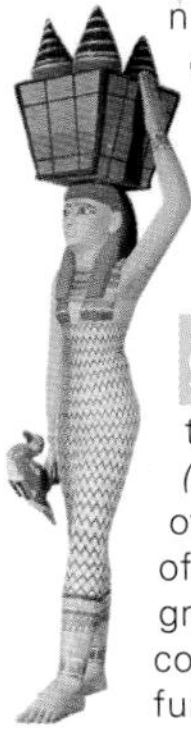
A Middle Kingdom model

9 Mask of Thuya

Discovered in 1905, the tomb of Yuya and Thuya *(see p40)* has always been overshadowed by the discovery of the tomb of their great-grandson, Tutankhamun. It contained many beautiful funerary artefacts including a striking funerary mask of gilded plaster with inlaid glass and quartz.

10 Fayoum Portraits

In Room 14 on the first floor are these life-like portraits dating from the period of Roman rule in Egypt (30 BC–395 AD). They represent some of the world's earliest portraiture. Painted on wooden boards during the subject's lifetime, they were at death laid over the face of the mummified corpse before it was placed into its sarcophagus.

A Fayoum portrait

Some of these items may be transferred to the new Grand Egyptian Museum under construction at Giza, due to open in 2015.

TOP 10 The Pyramids of Giza

Despite centuries of study, the Pyramids remain a mystery. There's their age: we are closer in time to the era of Jesus Christ than he was to the Pyramids. There's their size: for 4,000 years the Great Pyramid remained the tallest man-made structure ever built. There's the how: the Pyramids are precisely placed, their sides aligning to true north with only 3/60th a degree of error, while certain internal air shafts line up perfectly with celestial constellations. And, of course, there's the why: merely tombs for pharaohs or something much more?

Sound and Light Show

The Pyramids are best visited early in the morning, before the heat and crowds become too overwhelming.

Hawkers and touts at the Pyramids can be quite aggressive. Do not be intimidated.

There are plenty of shops and cafés in the small village by the entrance to the Sphinx.

• Map H2 • Sharia al-Ahram, Giza, 12 km (8 miles) SW of Cairo • 02 3383 8823 • Bus 355, 357 from Midan Tahrir • Giza Plateau open 8am–5pm (until 6pm in summer); Sound and Light Show (in English): 7:30pm (30 minutes later in summer) – schedules are subject to change, so check at ticket office near Sphinx or online at www.soundandlight.com.eg • Giza Plateau £E60; Solar Boat Museum £E50; Pyramid of Khufu £E100; Pyramid of Khafre £E35; Pyramid of Menkaure £E35

Top 10 Features

1. Giza Plateau
2. The Sphinx
3. Pyramid of Khufu (Cheops)
4. Pyramid of Khafre (Chepren)
5. Pyramid of Menkaure (Mycerinus)
6. Solar Boat Museum
7. Inside the Pyramids
8. Khafre's Valley Temple
9. Camel Rides
10. Sound and Light Show

1 Giza Plateau

Around 2600 BC the rocky Giza plateau *(above)* became the burial ground (necropolis) for Memphis, then the capital of Egypt. In less than a century during the Old Kingdom three successive generations built the three great Pyramids and associated structures.

2 The Sphinx

Its age is a point of contention, but the traditional view is that the Sphinx *(right)* was sculpted around 2500 BC by Khafre and that it is his face – now minus a nose – that fronts the leonine body. It also once had a beard, and parts of this are now in the Egyptian Museum and the British Museum.

3 Pyramid of Khufu (Cheops)

Also known simply as the Great Pyramid, this is the tallest and oldest of the trio. It was built during the reign of Khufu (2589–2566 BC) and originally stood 140 m (460 ft) high and measured 230 m (750 ft) along its base. These measurements are less now due to the removal of the outer casing of stone.

4 Pyramid of Khafre (Chephren)

Slightly smaller than Khufu's pyramid, the Pyramid of Khafre often seems bigger by virtue of being sited on higher ground. Its summit retains the smooth limestone casing that originally covered the whole of the three pyramids.

5 Pyramid of Menkaure (Mycerinus)

This pyramid's base area is less than a quarter of that of the other two, but its temples are more elaborate. This is perhaps a sign of the waning power of the pharaoh as well as a shift in priorities in funerary architecture.

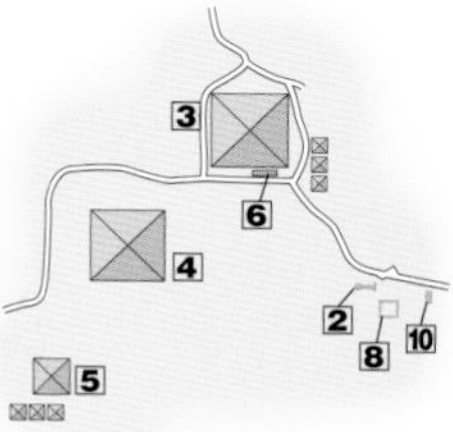

6 Solar Boat Museum

A pod-shaped structure by the Great Pyramid contains a full-size ancient Egyptian boat *(above)*, recovered from a pit sunk around the pyramid. It may have been intended to allow the pharaoh to accompany the sun-god on his daily journey across the heavens, hence the name.

9 Camel Rides

Local entrepreneurs offer camel rides near the Pyramids *(above)*. The site is small enough that you don't need a ride but it can be fun. Be prepared to haggle hard over the price.

10 Sound and Light Show

Every evening there are two one-hour shows in which the history of ancient Egypt is related by the "voice of the Sphinx" whilst lights play across the Pyramids.

7 Inside the Pyramids

Entering the Pyramids involves ascending and descending steeply-sloping, low-ceilinged passageways, and is not recommended for the claustrophobic.

8 Khafre's Valley Temple

Each pyramid was part of a greater funerary complex beginning with a valley temple. The remains of that of Khafre *(below)* are near the Sphinx.

Pyramid Evolution

The first tombs were mastabas (low, flat-topped buildings). The first pyramid, Djoser's Stepped Pyramid at Saqqara, was formed of six mastabas on top of each other. The first smooth-sided pyramid (at Meidum on the edge of the Fayoum Oasis) was achieved by filling in the steps of a stepped pyramid. The next stage was purpose-built smooth-sided pyramids, prototyped at Dahshur *(see p91)*.

TOP 10 Mosque of Al-Azhar

Al-Azhar was founded in AD 970 as the city's main mosque and centre of learning and to this day its institutions remain central to religious and political life in Egypt. Al-Azhar University is still one of the most revered centres of learning in the Sunni Islamic world, although teaching has long since left the mosque and now takes place in several modern campuses around the country. The mosque is a favourite venue for political demonstrations, often of an anti-government nature, particularly following noon prayers on a Friday.

View from the courtyard showing a minaret

Non-Muslims are welcome to visit the mosque but must be dressed appropriately: this means no shorts or bare shoulders. Women must cover their hair with a scarf and everybody must remove their shoes.

Avoid the mosque on Friday afternoons when the crowd is often fired up by political speeches.

There are plenty of cafés and coffee shops in the nearby Khan al-Khalili area.

- *Map J4*
- *Sharia al-Azhar, Al-Hussein district, Cairo*
- *Open 7:30am–7:30pm Mon–Thu & Sun; 7:30–11am, 3–5pm Fri. Official tourist visiting times: 9am–5pm (until 6pm in summer); closed to visitors Fri noon prayers.*

Top 10 Features

1. Gate of the Barbers
2. The Madrassas
3. Courtyard
4. Prayer Hall
5. The Minarets
6. Midan al-Hussein
7. Khan al-Khalili
8. Beit Zeinab Khatoun and Beit al-Harawi
9. Wikala of Al-Ghouri
10. Mosque of Sayyidna al-Hussein

1 Gate of the Barbers

Entrance to the mosque is via a double-arched gate *(below)*, dating from the 15th century, where students traditionally had their heads shaved, hence the name.

2 The Madrassas

Inside the main gate are two *madrassas* (places of religious study) dating from the early 14th century *(right)*. The *madrassa* on the left is usually open and has a beautiful ornate *mihrab* (niche indicating the direction of prayer towards Mecca).

3 Courtyard

Al-Azhar Mosque has undergone a series of enlargements and restorations throughout its history, and all styles and periods of history are represented in its architecture. The courtyard *(sahn)* is one of the oldest parts *(main image)*. Its arcades are carried on salvaged pre-Islamic columns.

For more on the etiquette of visiting mosques **see p119**

4 Prayer Hall

The large, carpeted alabaster-pillared prayer hall has five aisles and a transept that runs directly from the courtyard to the *mihrab (left)*.

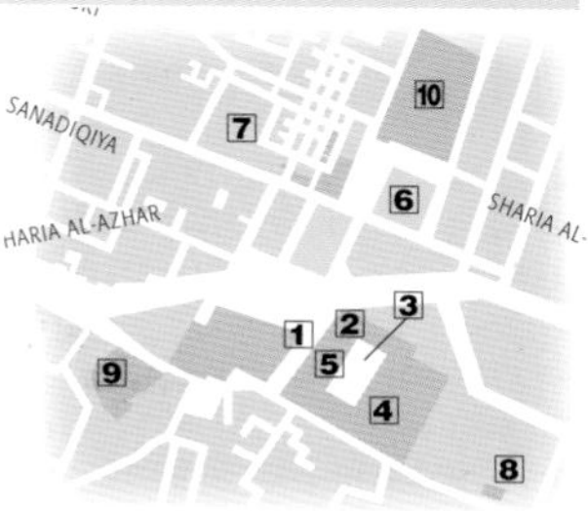

5 The Minarets

Al-Azhar has five imposing minarets. Its three main minarets overlooking the courtyard date, from north to south, from AD 1340, 1469 and 1510.

6 Midan al-Hussein

This square, on the opposite side of the main road from Al-Azhar mosque, is a major gathering place, particularly during holidays, feast days and saints days *(moulids)*.

7 Khan al-Khalili

Adjacent to Al-Azhar is Cairo's main souq area, Khan al-Khalili *(above)*. Its maze of narrow, medieval alleyways is crammed with small stalls and shops selling spices, perfumes, gold and silver.

9 Wikala of Al-Ghouri

Just west of Al-Azhar mosque is this 16th-century former merchants' hostel *(wikala)*. The beautifully restored structure now serves as the venue for performances by a troupe of whirling dervishes.

10 Mosque of Sayyidna al-Hussein

Just north of Al-Azhar is the holiest mosque in Egypt, which supposedly shelters one of the most sacred relics of Islam – the head of Al-Hussein, grandson of the Prophet Mohammed. Non-Muslims are not allowed to enter.

8 Beit Zeinab Khatoun and Beit al-Harawi

To the east of Al-Azhar mosque are two restored Ottoman-era houses *(beit)*, showing the fine domestic architecture that once filled the city *(below)*. They are now used for hosting cultural events.

City of Minarets

The Cairo skyline bears a distinctive signature composed of hundreds of minarets. The most beautiful of these, largely dating from the Mamluk period (1250–1517), have stonework adorned with intricate decorative carving. Many of the minarets can be climbed for superb views across the city rooftops.

TOP 10 Karnak

Even more so than the Pyramids of Giza, Karnak is Egypt's most important Pharaonic site. Throughout the Middle and New Kingdom eras, when ancient Egypt was at its pinnacle, Karnak was the country's powerbase. It was the home of the gods and the seat of the pharaoh and the priestly ruling caste. For over 1,300 years the complex was constantly expanded, and its scale is immense, incorporating countless courts, halls and temples. Almost every pharaoh of note has left their mark.

Pylon of the Temple of Khonsu

Excavations are ongoing, and only a part of the vast site is accessible.

Be sure to wear a hat and carry a bottle of water. Allow at least half a day to explore.

The Visitors' Centre has a scale model of ancient Karnak.

There are cafés and restaurants next to the plaza at the site entrance, and a café by the Sacred Lake.

- *Map Z4*
- *Sharia al-Karnak, 3 km (2 miles) NE of Luxor*
- *Open 6am–5pm (7am–6pm in summer)*
- *General site adm £E65*
- *Open-Air Museum adm £E25 (separate ticket required, which must be bought before entering the complex)*
- *Sound and Light Show: 7pm, 8:15pm, 9:30pm (also 10:45pm in summer); £E100; languages vary, check details on www.soundandlight.com.eg*

Top 10 Features

1. Avenue of Sphinxes
2. Precinct of Amun
3. Temple of Amun
4. Open-Air Museum
5. Temple of Khonsu
6. Sacred Lake
7. Cachette Court
8. Seventh and Eighth Pylons
9. Precinct of Montu
10. Sound and Light Show

1 Avenue of Sphinxes

The site is approached via a short avenue of sphinxes *(above)* that originally connected the entrance pylon with a dock fed by a canal from the Nile. On the south side of Karnak is another sphinx avenue, which connects with Luxor Temple *(see pp20–21)*.

2 Precinct of Amun

The Karnak complex has three main compounds. The grandest precinct, dedicated to Amun, lies at the centre, dominated by the huge Temple of Amun. It contains a Sacred Lake and a series of pylons arranged perpendicular to the main temple. The pylons lead to the adjacent Precinct of Mut, which is closed to visitors.

3 Temple of Amun

The heart of Karnak is the Temple of Amun *(below)*, spanning thirteen centuries. The scale is vast, consisting of a succession of pylons, courts, colonnades and chambers arranged along a central axis *(see pp18–19)*.

For more on the gods and goddesses of ancient Egypt **see p37**

Open-Air Museum 4

Situated within the Precinct of Amun, the museum contains a fine collection of statuary *(right)* and monuments discovered during an excavation of the Third Pylon of the Temple of Amun. A separate ticket is required for the museum.

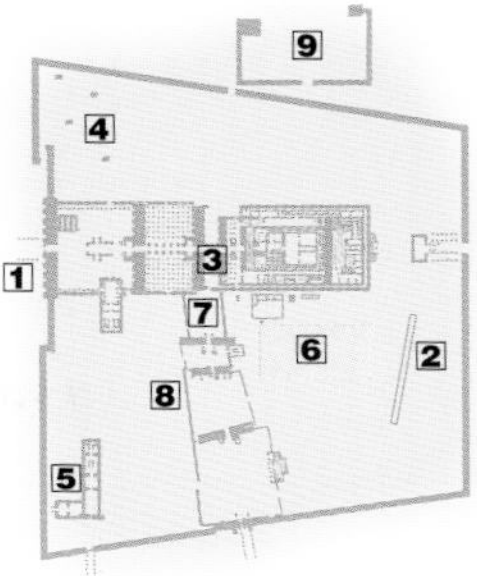

5 Temple of Khonsu

This small temple in the Precinct of Amun, dedicated to the son of Amun, was mostly built by Ramses II and IV. Next to it is a smaller temple to Opet, the hippopotamus goddess.

6 Sacred Lake

Priests purified themselves in the holy water of the Sacred Lake *(below)* before performing rituals in the temple. Nearby is a giant stone scarab of Khepri, god of the dawning sun.

7 Cachette Court

The Cachette Court gets its name from the discovery of a hoard of some 900 stone statues here, the finest of which are now in the Luxor and Cairo museums.

8 Seventh and Eighth Pylons

A succession of courts and pylons runs south from the Cachette Court. The first of these, the Seventh Pylon, is ascribed to Tuthmosis III, and two partial colossi of him sit in the courtyard beyond. The well-preserved Eighth Pylon was probably constructed during the reign of Hatshepsut.

9 Precinct of Montu

The warrior god Montu was the god of Karnak. His precinct, north of that of Amun, contains temples to both Montu and Amun. Both temples are currently closed to the public.

Sound and Light Show 10

A dramatized history of Karnak is related three times nightly with an accompanying light show *(right)*. It is viewed from a grandstand beside the Sacred Lake.

The Theban Triad

The three dominant Egyptian gods in the area of Thebes (modern-day Luxor) were Amun, the all-powerful god to whom Karnak is dedicated, his consort Mut and their son Khonsu. Together they form the Theban triad. Mut was said to swallow the sun in the evening (sunset) and to give birth to it again in the morning (sunrise).

Left **Carving inside the Great Festival Temple** Right **Wall carving on the Great Hypostyle Hall**

TOP 10 Karnak: Temple of Amun

1 First Pylon

The massive First Pylon makes a suitably magnificent entrance to Karnak. At 130 m (416 ft) in width, it is the largest pylon in Egypt. Look up to the right and in the doorjamb it is possible to make out inscriptions of Karnak's vital statistics and the distances to other temples in Upper Egypt, carved by Napoleonic surveyors.

2 Shrine of Seti II

Immediately inside the First Pylon on the left is the Shrine of Seti II. It is composed of three small chapels for the placing of the sacred barques (boats) of Amun, Mut and Khonsu. They each have niches at the rear that would once have contained statues of the deities.

3 Colossus of Ramses II

Ramses II was the great warrior pharaoh who built some of ancient Egypt's most spectacular monuments, including the Ramesseum *(see p100)* and the Sun Temple at Abu Simbel *(see pp30–31)*. His imposing pink-granite statue, with one of his daughters at his feet, stands in front of the Second Pylon.

4 Temple of Ramses III

This is a miniature version of Ramses III's grand temple at Medinat Habu *(see p100)*. Two colossi flank the entrance, which leads to a hall lined with pillars in the form of Ramses III, the last pharaoh to wield any substantial power in Egypt.

Temple of Ramses III

5 Great Hypostyle Hall

Karnak's stunning Hypostyle Hall is a forest of 134 immense columns, set out in rows. Each of the central 12 columns is 21 m (69 ft) tall and it takes six adults with outstretched arms to encircle each column. The immense hall would originally have been roofed and peopled with statues.

Colossus of Ramses II

6 Obelisks of Hatshepsut

Two rose-granite obelisks, 27 m (89 ft) high were erected by Hatshepsut. Only one stands, defaced and wrapped around by a wall, an act of revenge by her long-frustrated successor to the throne, Tuthmosis III. Smashed sections of the obelisk's twin lie around the temple.

7 Great Festival Temple

Built by Tuthmosis III, the Great Festival Temple has unusual tent pole-shaped columns whose capitals

Key Pharaohs who Ruled from Karnak

1. Tuthmosis I
2. Hatshepsut
3. Tuthmosis III
4. Amenhotep III
5. Tutankhamun
6. Horemheb
7. Ramses I
8. Seti I
9. Ramses II
10. Ramses III

The Temple Priests

Ancient Egyptian priests, such as those of Karnak, were known as "hem-netjer", literally "servants of the god or goddess", responsible for performing the daily rituals that regulated the workings of the universe. The high priest was responsible for the honouring of the god within its shrine. Twice daily the "cult" statue was bathed and clothed before receiving offerings of food and drink. Incense was burnt and holy water from the Sacred Lake scattered to show the purity of the offerings. Priests were not necessarily wholly religious – some were teachers; others attended to the economic organization of the temple. Although the Temple of Amun was the residence of the god, it also included workshops, libraries and administrative areas.

Statue of Amun
The god Amun became the most powerful of gods during the New Kingdom era when he was depicted as a human.

Relief depicting the god Thoth in the Temple of Amun

have blue and white chevrons. Saints painted on some columns are evidence of the hall's use as a church during early Christian times.

8 Botanical Garden

On the east side of the Great Festival Temple is a roofless enclosure known as the Botanical Garden for its painted reliefs of plants and animals. Beside this is a small roofed chamber from the time of Alexander the Great, who is shown in relief standing before Amun and other deities.

9 Chapels of the Hearing Ear

Straddling the main temple's enclosure wall at the rear of the complex are the ruined halls and colonnades of several shrines dedicated to lesser gods. These were where the general populace, who were excluded from the Precinct of Amun, came to have their petitions transmitted to the great Theban gods via intermediary deities.

10 Lateran Obelisk

Behind the Hearing Ear chapels is a pedestal on which once stood Egypt's tallest obelisk (31 m/102 ft). It was completed in the reign of Tuthmosis IV. Some 1,700 years later the Byzantine Emperor Constantius II (r. AD 337–361) had the obelisk moved to Rome, where it still stands in the Piazza di San Giovanni in Laterano.

TOP 10 Luxor Temple

Set close to the bank of the Nile and in the centre of the modern town, Luxor Temple is quite literally unmissable. It is an elegant, compact complex, as unlike Karnak, it is largely the work of a single pharaoh, Amenhotep III, with just a few additions made during the reign of Ramses II. The site was occupied by a Roman camp in the 3rd century AD but was subsequently abandoned and became engulfed in silt and sand on top of which a village was built. It remained thus until the late 19th century when excavations began.

Obelisk in front of the main pylon

Impressive by day, Luxor Temple is also supremely atmospheric by night when it is beautifully lit. Visit late in the afternoon, then stay until dusk, or come in the morning and return in the evening, since a ticket permits re-entry on the same day.

There are no refreshments sold on site, but water sellers congregate around the entrance to the temple, and there are cafés on the Corniche nearby.

- *Map Y2*
- *Corniche al-Nil, Luxor*
- *Open 6am–9pm (until 10pm in summer)*
- *General site adm £E50*

Top 10 Features

1. Avenue of Sphinxes
2. Obelisk
3. First Pylon
4. Court of Ramses II
5. Abu al-Haggag Mosque
6. Colonnade of Amenhotep III
7. Court of Amenhotep III
8. Hypostyle Hall
9. Roman Paintings
10. Inner Sanctum

1 Avenue of Sphinxes

Leading to the temple is a procession of sphinxes *(above)* that goes up to the Precinct of Mut at Karnak. Almost all of the route was deeply buried under the modern town but has now been uncovered.

2 Obelisk

Standing before the temple's main pylon are two seated colossi of Ramses II and a pink granite obelisk. The obelisk was originally one of a pair but the other was removed in the early 19th century and re-erected in the Place de la Concorde, Paris, as a gift to France.

3 First Pylon

The entrance is a 24-m (79-ft) high pylon *(main image)*, added by Ramses II, which serves as a poster for his achievements. It is decorated with scenes of his military triumphs, such as the Battle of Qadesh.

4 Court of Ramses II

Beyond the pylon, this court has a double row of papyrus-bud columns, interspersed with more statues of Ramses II *(below)*.

For more information on the gods and goddesses of ancient Egypt **see p37**

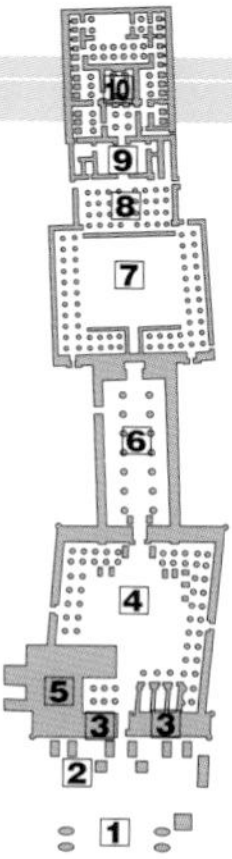

5 Abu al-Haggag Mosque

Perched on top of the colonnade of the Court of Ramses is this much rebuilt and beautifully restored 13th-century mosque *(left)* dedicated to Luxor's patron saint. It is all that is left of the village that was cleared to reveal the temple in the 1880s.

6 Colonnade of Amenhotep III

Guarded by more giant statues of Ramses II, the original part of the temple begins with a majestic avenue of 14 columns *(below)*. The walls here depict the annual Opet Festival.

7 Court of Amenhotep III

This court is noted for its double rows of towering papyrus-bundle columns. In 1989 a cache of 22 New Kingdom statues was discovered here, and they are now on display in the Luxor Museum.

8 Hypostyle Hall

The southern side of Amenhotep's fine court merges into a hypostyle hall with 32 more papyrus columns. Between the last two columns to the left of the central aisle is a Roman altar dedicated to Emperor Constantine.

9 Roman Paintings

Beyond the Hypostyle Hall are a series of small antechambers. In the first of these the Romans plastered over the Pharaonic reliefs, covering them with imperial cult paintings *(right)*.

10 Inner Sanctum

The heart of the temple is the Sanctuary of the Sacred Barque, where Amun's barque ended its journey from Karnak during the annual Opet Festival. Beyond this is a small damaged sanctuary that once housed a golden statue of Amun.

The Opet Festival

Once a year during the flood season, the Festival of Opet celebrated the pharaoh's rebirth as the son of Amun. Images of the Theban Triad *(see p17)* were carried from Karnak on boats (barques) to Luxor Temple. Luxor stages a recreation of the festival in November each year (check dates with the tourist office on 095 2373 294).

Top 10 Temple of Hatshepsut

This is the most intriguing of the temples and tombs on Luxor's West Bank, partly due to the breathtaking spectacle it presents – a series of sweeping terraces set against a vertiginous mountain backdrop – and partly because the temple was built for the only woman to reign over Egypt as pharaoh. When her husband Tuthmosis II died young, Hatshepsut became regent to her step-son Tuthmosis III, later usurping him altogether to take the crown for herself. She reigned from 1473 until 1458 BC.

Head of Hatshepsut

The West Bank becomes extremely hot and there is hardly any shade at Hatshepsut's temple, so visit as early in the day as possible when the sun is still low.

There is a handful of pricey stalls selling water, soft drinks and biscuits near the entrance to the temple site.

- *Map V2*
- *2 km (1 mile) NE of the West Bank ticket kiosk, Luxor*
- *Open 6am–5pm (until 6pm in summer)*
- *General site adm £E35; tickets are available at the entrance to the site*

Top 10 Features

1. Courtyard Approach
2. Courtyard Colonnade
3. Lower Terrace
4. Chapel of Anubis
5. Reliefs of Punt Expedition
6. Birth Colonnade
7. Chapel of Hathor
8. Statues of Hatshepsut
9. Upper Terrace
10. Temple of Montuhotep

1 Courtyard Approach

Missing from the reconstructed temple is the avenue of sphinxes and the gardens planted with myrrh trees; only the stumps of two 3,500-year-old trees remain near the site barriers.

2 Courtyard Colonnade

The lowest of the temple's colonnades depicts scenes of fish and birds being caught in nets and the queen's two great obelisks being transported from Aswan to Karnak.

3 Lower Terrace

Reached by a processional ramp, the Lower Terrace would, like the Courtyard below, once have been planted with trees. Vast and bare, the interest for visitors now lies in the colonnades at the rear and their carved reliefs.

4 Chapel of Anubis

On the Lower Terrrace, this chapel has brightly coloured murals, including a relief of Tuthmosis III making offerings to the sun god Ra-Harakhty *(below)*.

For more information on the gods and goddesses of ancient Egypt **see p37**

Reliefs of Punt Expedition 5

Splendid reliefs *(right)* depict Hatshepsut's journey on a trading expedition to the Land of Punt (present day Somalia), meeting with the king and queen of Punt and returning with lavish goods.

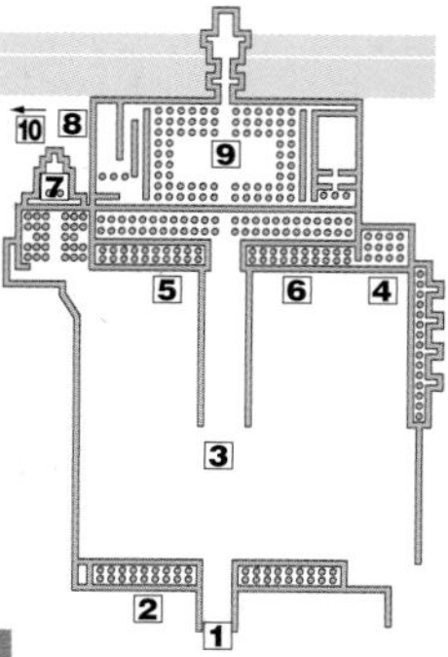

6 Birth Colonnade

Scenes along the Birth Colonnade delicately portray the divine birth of Hatshepsut, a sequence designed to legitimize the queen's claim to the throne.

7 Chapel of Hathor

This chapel is noted for its Hathor-headed columns *(above)*. At the back, there is a carved relief of Hathor in the form of a cow licking Hatshepsut's hand.

8 Statues of Hatshepsut

The columns of the portico around the Upper Terrace were decorated with statues of Hatshepsut represented as a male king with a beard *(left)*. Most were destroyed but some have been reconstructed.

Upper Terrace 9

On this level *(right)*, there are more reliefs, including oarsmen rowing the royal barque. At the rear is the Sanctuary of Amun, dug into the cliff behind the temple.

10 Temple of Montuhotep

The prototype for Hatshepsut's temple is the earlier Temple of Montuhotep II, which lies in ruins immediately adjacent to the north. Montuhotep was the first pharaoh to choose to be buried at Thebes.

Hatshepsut's Missing Mummy

When Howard Carter opened Hatshepsut's sarcophagus, he found out that it was empty. However, modern CT scans have revealed that a molar tooth, placed in a box bearing her cartouche, fits a socket in the jaw of an obese mummy that was discovered in tomb KV-60 in 1903. Could this prove to be the great woman pharaoh?

Top 10 Valley of the Kings

During the greatest period of ancient Egyptian history almost every pharaoh was buried here in tombs hewn into the rock and decorated with extraordinary art. To date, 63 tombs have been discovered and there may still be more to come, making this the richest archaeological site on earth. The numbers assigned to the tombs (given here in brackets) represent the order in which they were discovered, but a better way to approach the valley is to visit the tombs in the order in which they were constructed, as they are presented here. In this way it is possible to witness the flowering and eventual decline of ancient Egyptian tomb art.

View of the entrance to the Valley of the Kings

Begin at the Visitors' Centre, which has an excellent scale model of the valley. The tombs are opened in rotation, with around 12 accessible at any one time; six tombs is about as many as most people can visit in one trip.

There is a basic café–restaurant selling water, soft drinks and snacks at the entrance to the valley.

- *Map U2*
- *2 km (1 mile) N of the West Bank ticket kiosk, Luxor*
- *Open 6am–4pm (until 5pm in summer)*
- *www.thebanmappingproject.com*
- *For any three tombs adm £E80; Tutankhamun's tomb adm £E100; Tomb of Ramses VI adm £E50; tickets are available at the entrance to the site*

Top 10 Features

1. Tomb of Tuthmosis III (No.34)
2. Tomb of Amenhotep II (No.35)
3. Tomb of Tutankhamun (No.62)
4. Tomb of Horemheb (No.57)
5. Tomb of Ramses I (No.16)
6. Tomb of Seti I (No.17)
7. Tomb of Merneptah (No.8)
8. Tomb of Ramses III (No.11)
9. Tomb of Ramses IV (No.2)
10. Tomb of Ramses VI (No.9)

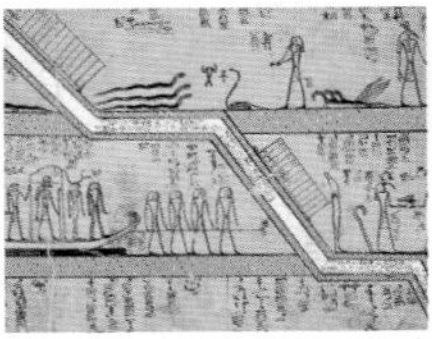

1 Tuthmosis III (No.34)

Tuthmosis III was one of the first pharaohs to be buried in the valley. His tomb is at the furthest end, burrowed high into the mountainside in an attempt to thwart thieves. The tomb decorations from this period are very crude, with figures rendered as stick people *(above)*.

2 Amenhotep II (No.35)

This is one of the deepest tombs in the valley, with 90 steps leading down to the various chambers. Amenhotep II ruled immediately after Tuthmosis III and this tomb has similarly basic wall paintings, as well as containing Amenhotep's sarcophagus.

3 Tutankhamun (No.62)

This is a very small tomb *(main image)*, but it is one of the most visited thanks to the story of its discovery by Howard Carter *(see opposite)*. All of the treasures have been removed and visitors must be content with seeing the king's mummy, which lies inside a gilded coffin.

4 Horemheb (No.57)

The introduction of bas-relief in this tomb, in which figures are carved out before painting, shows an advance in tomb art *(above)*. Not all figures are finished and it is fascinating to see the work in various stages of completion.

5 Ramses I (No.16)

Ramses I ruled only for a single year and his tomb is correspondingly modest in size. It has the shortest entrance corridor in the valley leading to a small burial chamber. However, the colours of the tomb paintings remain particularly vibrant *(above)*.

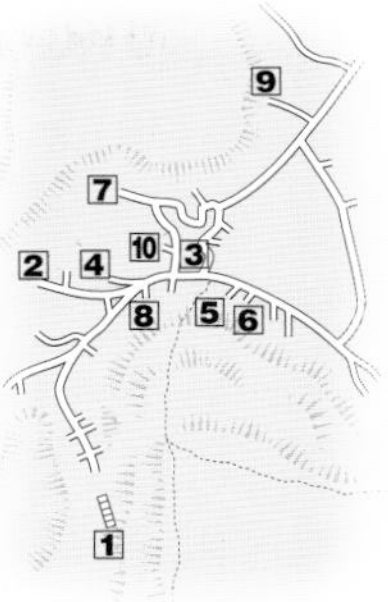

6 Seti I (No.17)

If you visit only one tomb, it should be this one – the longest, deepest and most lavishly decorated tomb in the valley. The vaulted burial chamber boasts a beautiful ceiling, showing the constellations surrounded by a line-up of deities *(below)*.

8 Ramses III (No.11)

This is also known as the "Tomb of the Harpists" after the bas-relief of two musicians. Unusually for a royal tomb, its colourful reliefs include scenes of everyday Egyptian life.

9 Ramses IV (No.2)

Ramses III was the last of the great pharaohs. The quality of the craftsmanship in the tomb of his successor is noticeably poorer than those that came before.

10 Ramses VI (No.9)

This tomb has very dense decoration *(right)*, representing sacred texts and imagery, central to which is the voyage of the sun god Ra through the underworld and his victorious reemergence in the morning.

7 Merneptah (No.8)

One of the many sons of Ramses II, Merneptah's tomb almost equals that of Seti I for grandeur. This is the first tomb in which the axis is completely straight, terminating in a tomb chamber containing the pharaoh's magnificent granite sarcophagus.

Wonderful Things

Archaeologist Howard Carter had been digging in the Valley of the Kings for five seasons. His backer Lord Carnarvon was on the point of stopping the funding when on 4 November 1922 Carter discovered some steps. Three weeks later the pair broke through a second sealed door that allowed Carter to peer through into an undisturbed tomb. Asked by Carnarvon if he could see anything, Carter replied, "Yes, wonderful things".

For more information on the pharaohs of ancient Egypt **see pp34–5**

Top 10 Cruising the Nile

After disembarking their ocean liner at Alexandria, the 19th-century tourist would board a train for Cairo where they would hire a boat at the port of Bulaq. They would then make their way in a leisurely fashion down the Nile stopping off at each archaeological site along the way. The journey would take about 10 days, ending at Aswan, where a cataract rendered any further progress south impossible. That same journey can be made again today and remains by far the best way to experience the country. More usual are four- or seven-day cruises stopping at the major monuments of Upper (southern) Egypt.

A flotilla of feluccas on the Nile at Luxor

The number and variety of boats is overwhelming and it is advisable to do some research before booking. Itineraries are generally the same and the differences between cruisers lie in the quality of service and facilities on board.

From the 1980s until 2012, boats were not allowed to sail through Middle Egypt. Now the route is open again, and some high-end cruises make the 10-day journey to Luxor or the 14-day journey to Aswan.

All meals are usually included in the cost of the package but alcoholic drinks are put on a tab that has to be settled at the end of the cruise.

Top 10 Features

1. The Route
2. The Itinerary
3. The Boats
4. Feluccas
5. Steamers
6. Dahabiyyas
7. Life On Board
8. Life on the Nile
9. Death on the Nile
10. Cruising Lake Nasser

1 The Route

The most popular route departs from Luxor and takes three days to reach Aswan, where it turns around for the return trip. It is also possible to cruise from Cairo to Aswan.

2 The Itinerary

As well as the sites at Luxor and Aswan, cruises all stop at Esna, Edfu and Kom Ombo, each of which has a Pharaonic temple. Full-day excursions are typically offered to Abu Simbel on Lake Nasser.

3 The Boats

There are over 300 cruise boats on the Nile *(below)*, varying in size from those with just a handful of cabins to vessels capable of carrying several hundred people. Nearly all have air-conditioned cabins with en-suite bathrooms.

For more information on the temples of Esna, Edfu and Kom Ombo **see pp39 & 107**

4 Feluccas

The cheapest way of sailing the Nile is to charter one of the small single-sailed boats that scud about the river *(left)*. These are hired in Aswan, usually for a three-day, two-night journey to Edfu. Sleeping arrangements are a blanket, and meals are part of the deal.

5 Steamers

These were the boats that cruised the Nile in the early years of the 20th century. Now meticulously restored, they provide a more characterful, though still affordable, option than the standard Nile cruiser.

6 Dahabiyyas

The most exclusive option is a berth on a dahabiyya *(below)*, a newly-built replica of the twin-sail boat that used to cruise the Nile in the 19th century. Each carries between 5 and 20 people in five-star comfort.

7 Life On Board

Most cruise packages include an Egyptologist, who delivers lectures on ancient Egyptian history and acts as a guide on visits to the monuments. Parties and folkloric events are organized as evening entertainment.

8 Life on the Nile

Part of the appeal of a cruise is the opportunity to observe rural life on the shores of the river *(right)* – water buffalo bathing in the shallows, villagers at work in the cane fields and an abundance of water birds.

9 Death on the Nile

Agatha Christie's 1937 murder mystery is recommended reading on a Nile cruise as it takes place on board a Nile steamer and at the Pharaonic sites of Upper Egypt. It was written in part during a stay at Aswan's Old Cataract Hotel *(see pp53 &131)*.

10 Cruising Lake Nasser

As an alternative to the Nile cruise, a number of boats cruise Lake Nasser, sailing from moorings at the High Dam, south of Aswan, to the great Temple of Abu Simbel, and stopping at several little-visited desert temples en route.

Thomas Cook & Son

The popularization of Nile cruising, and of mass tourism to Egypt, is largely due to John Mason Cook, son of Thomas Cook. In the 1880s Cooks Ltd began tours to Egypt and invested heavily in the country's infrastructure and marketing. They had a network of "tourist stations" along the Nile offering conveniences from hotels to post offices to doctors.

For more information on boats and cruise operators on the Nile **see p133**

Top 10 Temple of Philae

Philae is the most picturesque of all Egypt's temples, thanks to its site – it sits on a Nile island reached by small motor launch. This Ptolemaic (Graeco-Roman) era temple is devoted to Isis, whose cult was to survive into early Christian times. After the building of the Aswan Dam (1898–1902), the island's temples were submerged for a part of each year. With the building of the High Dam (1969–71), the temples were relocated to nearby Agilika Island, which was landscaped to match the original site.

Tourist boat arriving at Philae from Aswan

If you are not travelling as part of a group, you can negotiate a taxi or rent a bicycle from Aswan to the Shallal dock, which is where the boats to Philae depart from.

There is a small café selling drinks and snacks on the island.

- *Map C5*
- *Agilika Island, S of Aswan*
- *Reached by taxi (or bicycle) from Aswan*
- *Open 7am–4pm (until 5pm in summer)*
- *Sound and Light Show: 6:30pm, 7:45pm, 9pm in winter; 7pm, 8:15pm, 9:30pm in summer*
- *Languages vary, so check schedules on www.soundandlight.com.eg*
- *General site adm £E50*
- *Sound and Light Show £E75*

Top 10 Features

1. Kiosk of Nectanebo
2. Colonnaded Courtyard
3. Temple of Isis
4. The Sanctuary
5. The Birth House
6. The Osiris Rooms
7. Hadrian's Gate
8. Temple of Hathor
9. Kiosk of Trajan
10. Sound and Light Show

1 Kiosk of Nectanebo

Boats drop visitors at a double stairway that leads up to the Kiosk of Nectanebo *(above)*, a small structure erected during the 4th century BC that acts as a gateway to the site.

2 Colonnaded Courtyard

Beyond the kiosk is an elongated courtyard flanked by colonnades. The west colonnade (to the left) has columns on which every capital is different and a rear wall punctuated by windows overlooking the water. The east colonnade is interrupted by a series of ruined structures.

3 Temple of Isis

The centrepiece of Philae is this beautiful, small temple built over several hundred years by Ptolemaic and Roman rulers *(main image and below)*. It is fronted by an ancient Egyptian pylon and two stone lions.

4 The Sanctuary

Beyond a second pylon, a hypostyle hall leads to vestibules that culminate in the innermost holy sanctuary, containing a stone pedestal that once supported the goddess Isis's barque.

The Graeco-Romans were also known as the Ptolemies, after the founder of the dynasty, Ptolemy I

5 The Birth House

The colonnaded Birth House *(left)* is where the pharaohs legitimized their rule as mortal descendants of Horus by taking part in rituals celebrating the god's birth. At the bottom of the rear wall are scenes of Isis giving birth to Horus in the marshes.

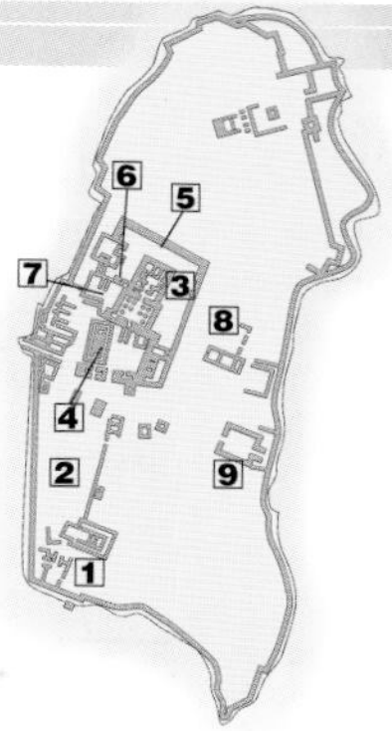

6 The Osiris Rooms

If the caretaker can be persuaded to unlock the way (with a tip), some upper rooms with reliefs depicting the resurrection of Osiris after his dismemberment by Seth *(see p37)* can be visited.

7 Hadrian's Gate

West of the temple is a small vestibule dedicated by the Roman emperor, inscribed with the date 24 August AD 394. Above the lintel, Hadrian is depicted presenting himself before a pantheon of ancient Egyptian deities.

8 Temple of Hathor

East of the main building is a small, ruinous temple, which still has two columns topped with Hathor heads, as well as a fine relief depicting musicians with the dwarf god Bess playing a harp.

9 Kiosk of Trajan

This imposing kiosk *(below)* was built around AD 100 by the Roman emperor Trajan and served as a royal landing for the temple. It combines Roman architecture with Pharaonic detailing.

10 Sound and Light Show

Of all Egypt's sound and light shows, the one at Philae is the best *(above)*. It consists of a one-hour floodlit tour through the ruins and is a highly atmospheric experience.

The Cult of Isis

Isis was the goddess of magic, and no ancient Egyptian cult lasted longer or spread further than hers. She became identified with women, sex and purity, and Isis worship spread throughout the Roman empire, with her cult temples appearing as far as what is now Hungary. For the first two centuries of Christianity's history, Isis was Christianity's main rival. It is possible that Christianity's cult of the Virgin was nurtured as a way of winning over Isis worshippers.

TOP 10 Abu Simbel

Carved out of a mountainside in the 13th century BC, Ramses II's stupendous Sun Temple at Abu Simbel was dedicated to three of Egypt's pre-eminent deities – Amun of Thebes, Ptah of Memphis and Ra-Harakhty of Heliopolis, but it is principally a monument to the might of the pharaoh. Located at the southernmost tip of ancient Egypt's borders, the four colossal statues of Ramses that front the temple gaze towards enemy territory as a warning to any who might approach.

Entrance to the Temple of Hathor

Abu Simbel is offered as an optional extra on most Nile cruises. Alternatively, most hotels in Aswan organize excursions by minibus, which generally leave at 4:30am and return on the same day. You can also fly to Abu Simbel from Aswan.

There are small shops and cafés in the town of Abu Simbel, a 20-minute walk from the temples.

- *Map B6*
- *Lake Nasser, 280 km (174 miles) S of Aswan*
- *Site open 7am–4pm (until 5pm in summer)*
- *Sound and Light Show: 6pm, 7pm, 8pm (in multiple languages via headsets)*
- *www.soundandlight.com.eg*
- *General site adm £E100*
- *Sound and Light Show £E75*

Top 10 Features

1. Lake Nasser
2. Visitors' Centre
3. The Colossi
4. Statue of Ra-Harakhty
5. Hypostyle Hall Reliefs
6. Ramses Pillars
7. Inner Sanctuary
8. The Sun Ceremony
9. Temple of Hathor
10. Sound and Light Show

1 Lake Nasser

Lake Nasser was formed with the completion of the High Dam in 1971. The water stretches south of the dam for nearly 500 km (300 miles) into Sudan. With a surface area of 6,000 sq km (3,700 sq miles) the lake is the world's largest reservoir.

3 The Colossi

Ramses II had his temple adorned with four gigantic colossi fashioned in his likeness *(main image)*. Each of the complete seated figures (one lost its upper torso in an earthquake in 27 BC) is more than 20 m (65 ft) in height.

2 Visitors' Centre

Like Philae, the temples at Abu Simbel were rescued from the rising waters of Lake Nasser. The Visitors' Centre contains an exhibition telling the story of the move, with diagrams, photographs and models.

4 Statue of Ra-Harakhty

Above the entrance to the temple is a statue of the falcon-headed sun god Ra-Harakhty *(left)*. At the top of the temple are the remains of a frieze of baboons worshipping the rising sun.

For more information on Lake Nasser **see pp108–13**

5 Hypostyle Hall Reliefs

The southern wall of the Hypostyle Hall depicts the Battle of Qadesh (c.1275 BC) *(above)*, in which the pharaoh leads his army in a defeat of the Hittites on the River Orontes in what is now Syria.

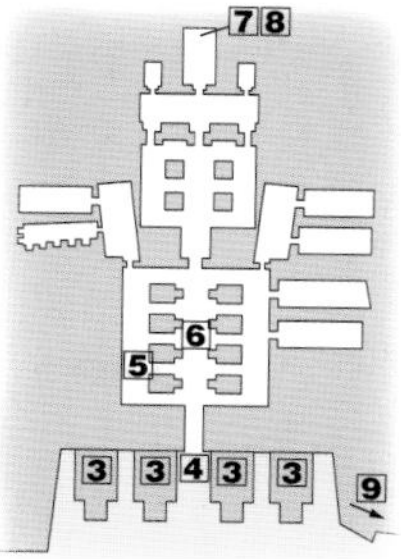

6 Ramses Pillars

The Hypostyle Hall has twin rows of four pillars fronted by 10-m (33-ft) statues of Ramses in Osiride form carrying crook and flail *(above)*.

7 Inner Sanctuary

A second pillared hall leads to a sanctuary at the rear of the temple, where there are four statues representing Ptah, Ramses II, Amun-Ra and Ra-Harakhty.

9 Temple of Hathor

Beside the Sun Temple is a temple dedicated to the goddess Hathor, built by Ramses II to honour his wife Nefertari *(below)*. The façade alternates colossi of the pharaoh and his queen. Inside is a hypostyle hall with Hathor-headed pillars.

8 The Sun Ceremony

The Sun Temple is aligned so that on 22 February and on 22 October every year (traditionally considered Ramses' birthday and coronation date, respectively), the first rays of the rising sun illuminate the sanctuary cult statues of Amun-Ra, Ra-Harakhty and Ramses II, while Ptah stays in shadow *(see p62)*.

10 Sound and Light Show

Set to music, this impressive show includes projections onto the temples showing how they once looked.

Rescue by UNESCO

In the 1960s, as the rising waters of Lake Nasser threatened to engulf the temples at Abu Simbel, UNESCO engineers cut them from the mountain in sections and reassembled the pieces to front an artificial mountain 210 m (700 ft) behind and 65 m (213 ft) above their original position.

Left **Tuthmosis III** Centre **First Intermediate Period fresco** Right **Early Dynastic ivory carving**

Top 10 Periods of Ancient Egyptian History

1 Early Dynastic Period (3100–2890 BC)

There is evidence of human activity in the Western Desert as far back as 8000 BC, but what we regard as ancient Egypt began in 3100 BC with the unification of Upper (southern) and Lower (northern) Egypt by King Narmer (also known as Menes), who created a capital at Memphis.

Middle Kingdom statuette

2 Old Kingdom (2686–2181 BC)

Also known as the Age of the Pyramids, successive dynasties of kings raised a chain of pyramids, the greatest of which were the trio at Giza *(see pp12–13)*. Subsequently, poor harvests depleted the royal coffers, which led to a decline in royal power, signified by a decrease in the size of pyramids.

3 First Intermediate Period (2181–2055 BC)

During this unstable period of ancient Egyptian history there were numerous ephemeral kings. The weakening of centralized power led to the establishment of local dynasties, notably at Herakleopolis in the Fayoum Oasis and Thebes in the south.

Old Kingdom relief with Egyptian scribes

4 Middle Kingdom (2055–1650 BC)

The powerful warlord Montuhotep II conquered the north to reunite the country with Thebes (modern-day Luxor) as its new capital, which grew into a major metropolis. Across the river, the first tombs and funerary temples were constructed at the foot of the Theban Hills on the west bank of the Nile.

5 Second Intermediate Period (1650–1550 BC)

Migrants from lands north of Egypt, referred to as Hyksos, assumed control and allied with Nubia to dominate southern Egypt. The country became subject to intermittent civil war.

6 New Kingdom (1550–1069 BC)

With the reunification of north and south and the expulsion of the Hyksos, Egypt entered a Golden Age, expanding its rule into Asia Minor and as far as the Euphrates. Captured treasures enriched the royal powerbase at Karnak, seat of the mightiest pharaohs including Ramses II.

Preceding pages **Temple of Hatshepsut at Deir al-Bahri in Thebes**

7 Third Intermediate Period (1069–715 BC)

The New Kingdom gave way to four centuries of disunity and foreign infiltration, with Egypt again divided into north (ruled from Tanis in the Delta) and south (ruled by the priests of Karnak) and subject to invasion by Libyans and Nubians.

8 Late Period (747–332 BC)

The Late Period began with the Assyrian invasion of Egypt, followed by the Persians in 525 BC. The Persians ruled for 200 years interrupted only by the short-lived 30th Dynasty of Egyptian pharaohs (380–343 BC), the last native rulers until the Revolution of 1952.

Late Period sarcophagus

9 Graeco-Roman Period (332–30 BC)

In 332 BC the Macedonian king Alexander the Great "liberated" Egypt from the Persians and founded his new capital, Alexandria, on the Mediterranean. He was succeeded by his trusted general Ptolemy, who founded a dynasty that ruled for 275 years ending with the dramatic death of the last of the Ptolemies, Cleopatra VII, lover of Julius Caesar and Marc Antony.

10 After the Pharaohs

With the defeat and suicide of Cleopatra in 30 BC, Egypt became part of the Roman empire. It remained under the rule of Rome, followed by that of Constantinople, capital of the Eastern Roman empire, until the arrival of conquering Arab armies in AD 640.

Top 10 Kings and Queens of Ancient Egypt

1. **Narmer (c.3100 BC)**
The king who started 30 dynasties of ancient Egyptian royalty.

2. **Djoser (2667–2648 BC)**
Djoser's architect Imhotep built the Step Pyramid at Saqqara, the world's oldest stone monument.

3. **Khufu (2589–2566 BC)**
A ruthless pharaoh, but celebrated as the builder of the Great Pyramid at Giza.

4. **Montuhotep II (2055–2004 BC)**
Reunited Egypt to initiate the Middle Kingdom.

5. **Ahmose (1550–1525 BC)**
Defeated the Hyksos to reunite Egypt once again and start the greatest period of Pharaonic history.

6. **Hatshepsut (1473–1458 BC)**
Egypt's only woman pharaoh and builder of a striking mortuary temple at Thebes.

7. **Tuthmosis III (1479–1425 BC)**
A military genius whose victories expanded the Egyptian empire to its furthest extents.

8. **Akhenaten (1352–1336 BC)**
Labelled as the "Heretic King" due to his attempts to embrace monotheism.

9. **Ramses II (1279–1213 BC)**
Ramses II's 66-year reign saw royal construction on a huge scale, notably at Abu Simbel.

10. **Cleopatra (51–30 BC)**
Cleopatra VII's death brought to an end 3,070 years of ancient Egyptian history.

Left **Temple of Dendara, near Qena** Right **Tomb painting of a scene from the Book of the Dead**

Top 10 Ancient Egyptian Culture and Myths

Cartonnage depicting the goddess Maat

1 Religious Life

For the ancient Egyptians, the universe was composed of dualities – fertile and barren, life and death, order and chaos – held in a state of equilibrium by the goddess Maat. To maintain this balance they built enormous temples dedicated to the gods.

2 Hieroglyphs

Hieroglyph means "sacred carved letter" and refers to the beautiful pictorial script used by the ancient Egyptians. Hieroglyphs can convey complex information. They can be read right to left, left to right or top to bottom.

Hieroglyphs

3 The Cult Temple

At the centre of every settlement was a cult temple. These temples served as a storehouse of divine power, maintained by the priests. The temple was also an economic and political centre employing large numbers of the local community and serving as a town hall, medical centre and college.

4 The Mortuary Temple

In addition to the local cult temples, each pharaoh also built a mortuary temple to serve as a place where, following his death, offerings could be made for his soul. In the Old and Middle Kingdoms the temples were attached to tombs but by around 1500 BC the tombs were separate and hidden away to foil robbers.

5 Burial Traditions

The ancient Egyptians believed in an eternal after-life and they developed a complex funerary cult aimed at maintaining their life after death. This involved preserving the body through a process of mummification. The tombs of the deceased were also stocked with everything that might be needed in the afterlife.

6 Mummification

The earliest mummies were probably accidental. True mummification began in the Fourth Dynasty. Special priests first removed the internal organs, which were stored in canopic jars, except for the heart, which remained in place to be weighed in the afterlife. Then the corpse was dried out and wrapped in linen.

7 Tomb Paintings

As a guarantee against a successful journey into the afterlife, ritual images and texts were used to decorate the tomb. These included scenes from the *Book of the Dead*, which contained instructions to help the deceased to pass safely through obstacles in the afterlife.

8 Mythology
Ancient Egyptian religion was a complex belief system involving a great number of deities originally based on aspects of the natural world. Over time different localities developed many and varied myths relating to their own deities.

9 The Creation Myth
In the beginning there was nothing but the sea of chaos, named Nun. Then Atum thought himself into being, sneezing to create Shu and Tefnut. Shu and Tefnut gave birth to two children: Geb, the earth, and Nut, the sky, who in turn gave birth to the stars.

10 Osiris and Isis
Osiris was murdered by his jealous brother Seth, who cut up the body scattering it all over Egypt. Osiris's wife Isis collected up the pieces and put him back together again as the first mummy. Brought back to life, Osiris became lord and judge of the dead.

Tomb painting of the gods Osiris and Atum

Top 10 Gods and Goddesses

1 Amun
Powerful Theban deity whose cult centre was at Karnak. When combined with Ra as Amun-Ra, he became king of the gods.

2 Anubis
Jackal-headed god of embalmers and guardian of the Underworld.

3 Hathor
Goddess of love, pleasure and beauty, who is often represented as a cow.

4 Horus
Usually represented with the head of a falcon, Horus is the god with whom all living pharaohs were identified.

5 Isis
Daughter of Geb, god of the Earth, and of Nut, Isis is the goddess of magic, whose cult centre was at Philae.

6 Nut
Goddess of the sky and a symbol of resurrection and rebirth, Nut was pictured as arched on her toes with her fingertips over the earth.

7 Osiris
God of the Underworld who granted all life, including the fertile flooding of the Nile River.

8 Ra
Pre-eminent form of the sun god, portrayed as a falcon-headed figure with the sun's disc resting on his head.

9 Seth
The god of the desert, storms and chaos is depicted with the head of an unknown creature with a curved snout and square ears.

10 Thoth
Ibis-headed god of wisdom and patron of scribes.

Left **Detail of a relief in Medinat Habu** Right **Temple of Seti I, Abydos**

TOP 10 Temples

Statues of Ramses II as Osiris, Ramesseum

1 Ramesseum

Ramses II, ruler of Egypt in the 19th Dynasty, built his mortuary temple, the Ramesseum, on the west bank of the Nile at Thebes as a statement of his everlasting greatness and to impress his subjects. Although there is very little left standing of the huge complex, what remains is still striking. It once had an 18-m (60-ft) high colossus of Ramses, parts of which now lie scattered around the site *(see p100)*.

2 Temple of Seti I, Abydos

Built during Seti I's reign (1294–1279 BC), this is one of the most intact temples in Egypt and has some of the finest decoration and bas-reliefs, many of which have retained their original colour. It is situated in Abydos, which was once a huge walled town and the cult centre of Osiris (god of the dead) and was regarded as the holiest of Egyptian towns in Pharaonic times. Due to its distance from the main tourist centres, it is a less visited site *(see p107)*.

3 Medinat Habu

Second in size only to Karnak, Medinat Habu was built by Ramses III in Thebes. It is dominated by the vast mortuary temple of Ramses III, modelled on Ramses II's Ramesseum. The complex also includes the remains of Ramses's royal palace. Often overlooked by tourists, this magnificent and haunting structure is definitely worth a visit *(see p100)*.

4 Temple of Horus, Edfu

Situated between Luxor and Aswan, the Temple of Horus at Edfu dates from 237 BC, when Egypt was ruled by the successors of Alexander the Great. These rulers copied earlier temples, preserving the architectural traditions of their Pharaonic predecessors, as can be seen in this vast structure, the most intact of all Egypt's temples *(see p107)*.

Temple of Horus at Edfu

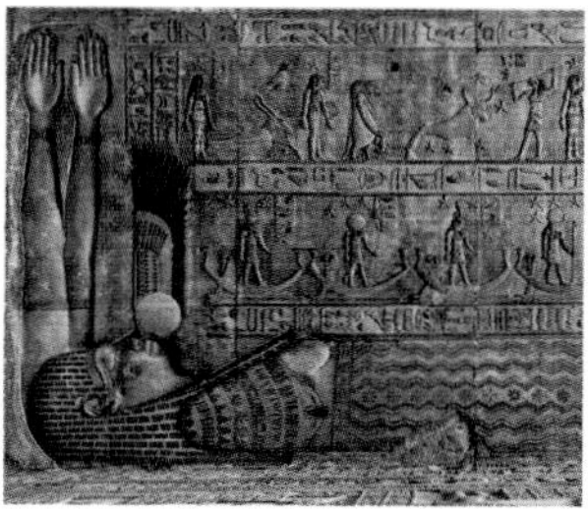
Detail of carved ceiling, Temple of Dendara

5 Dendara

Due to its location a little off the normal tourist trail near Qena, Dendara receives far fewer visitors than it deserves. Like the temple at Edfu, the temple at Dendara dates from the Graeco-Roman era. Dedicated to the goddess Hathor, it is remarkably well preserved and imitates typical Pharaonic temple architecture *(see p107)*.

6 Karnak

As well as being Egypt's most magnificent temple complex, Karnak is also one of Egypt's oldest Pharaonic sites. It started with humble beginnings during the 11th Dynasty, and was added to and expanded by every pharaoh over the course of 1,300 years until the 20th Dynasty. It contains many different courts, halls and temples. At the heart of the vast complex lies the Temple of Amun, dedicated to the king of gods *(see pp16–19)*.

7 Luxor Temple

Begun by Amenhotep III in the 18th Dynasty and added to by Ramses II in the 19th Dynasty, Luxor Temple is a perfect example of ancient Egyptian temple architecture. Located in the centre of modern Luxor town, it is easily accessible *(see pp20–21)*.

8 Temple of Hatshepsut

Hatshepsut was Egypt's only female pharaoh and her mortuary temple at Deir al-Bahri in Thebes was designed by her architect Senenmut in the 18th Dynasty. Partly hewn out of rock, it rises from the desert plain in a series of striking terraces. It is extraordinary in appearance and unlike any other surviving ancient Egyptian structure *(see pp22–3)*.

9 Philae

Centre of the cult of Isis, Philae is a comparatively late temple complex, dating from the Graeco-Roman period. It is a favourite with visitors thanks to a beautiful location on its own island in the Nile *(see pp28–9)*.

10 Abu Simbel

Ramses II (1279–1213 BC) built the spectacular Sun Temple at Abu Simbel. Due to the four colossi carved in his image that front the temple, he is the most famous of all pharaohs, with the exception perhaps of Tutankhamun *(see pp30–31)*.

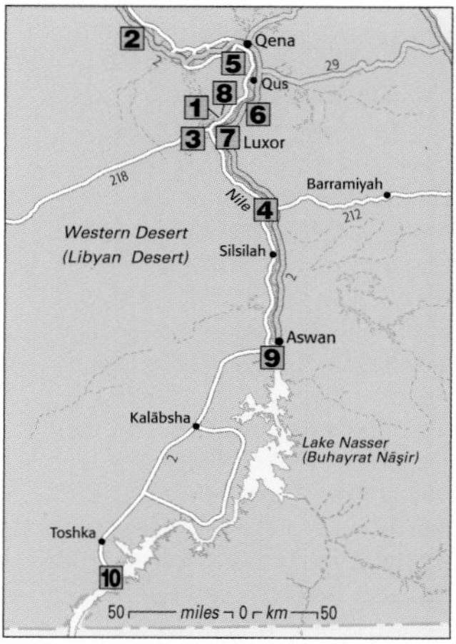

Engraving of Auguste Mariette's discovery of the Serapeum at Saqqara

Top 10 Milestones in Egyptology

Painting of Belzoni at a temple entrance

1 The Great Belzoni

Born in Padua, Italy, Giovanni Battista Belzoni (1778–1823) toured Europe as a circus strongman. Arriving in Egypt he was employed by the British consul to collect antiquities. He discovered several tombs at Thebes, including that of Seti I.

2 Decoding the Rosetta Stone (1822)

Discovered in 1799, this fragment from a large stele contained a decree written in two hieroglyphic scripts and in Greek. Through a comparison of the texts, Frenchman Jean-François Champollion was able to decipher ancient Egyptian hieroglyphs.

3 Mariette and the Serapeum (1851)

Frenchman Auguste Mariette was one of the first Egyptologists. Spotting a half-buried sphinx at Saqqara he commenced excavations that ultimately led to the discovery of the Serapeum, the burial place of the sacred Apis bulls.

4 The Deir al-Bahri Cache (1881)

The search for a stray goat led Ahmed Abdel Rassul down a shaft and into a chamber filled with sarcophagi. He kept the find quiet and for years his family leaked antiquities onto the market. When finally rumbled, officials took possession of the cache, which included the bodies of Ramses II and III and Tuthmosis I–III.

5 The Karnak Cachette (1903)

Workmen excavating in front of the Seventh Pylon at Karnak uncovered fragments of a colossal statue of Seti I. As they removed these, other statues could be seen. Some 751 items were eventually recovered, the largest find of statues ever made.

6 Yuya and Thuya (1905)

The first decade of the 20th century was a bumper time for discoveries in the Valley of the Kings, notably American Theodore Davies' discovery of the treasure-filled tomb of Yuya and Thuya, the parents of Queen Tiye, wife of Amenhotep III.

7 The Thutmose Gallery (1912)

Archaeologists digging at Tell al-Amarna *(see p107)* found a ruined house identified as belonging to the sculptor Thutmose in the 14th century BC. It was found to contain sculptures carved in a variety of stones.

8 The Tomb of Tutankhamun (1922)

This is the greatest archaeological find ever: a complete, undisturbed burial of a New Kingdom pharaoh, containing treasures to fill a whole museum. For more on the finding of the tomb see page 25.

9 The Luxor Statue Cache (1989)

One of the greatest finds of recent years was the discovery of a large group of statues beneath a court at Luxor Temple. Dating from the New Kingdom era, these include some of the finest examples of Pharaonic art ever found.

10 Underwater Discoveries off Alexandria (1990s–present)

Since the early 1990s two teams of divers headed by two French archaeologists have been diving off Alexandria. They have identified stone blocks that once made up the Pharos Lighthouse, one of the lost Seven Wonders of the ancient world, and have discovered submerged ruins marking the site of Cleopatra's palace and temple complex.

Howard Carter at the coffin of Tutankhamun

Top 10 Treasures Outside Egypt

1 The Rosetta Stone

Handed over by the French to the British as a spoil of war in 1801, this now resides in the British Museum, London.

2 The Zodiac Ceiling

This ceiling from the temple at Dendara is housed in the Louvre in Paris.

3 Bust of Nefertiti

Discovered at Abydos, this beautiful bust is displayed at the Altes Museum in Berlin.

4 Sarcophagus of Seti I

Removed from the Valley of the Kings by Belzoni, this is now at the Sir John Soane's Museum in London.

5 Temple of Dendur

Given to the USA in thanks for its financial contribution to the saving of Abu Simbel, this is on display at the Metropolian Museum in New York.

6 The Great Sphinx's Beard from Giza

Fragments are in both the Egyptian Museum, Cairo and the British Museum, London.

7 Statue of Ramses II

The superb collection of Egyptology in Italy's Turin Museum includes a statue of a youthful Ramses II.

8 Alabaster Statue of King Pepi II

The Brooklyn Museum in New York possesses an alabaster statue of King Pepi II.

9 Statue of Hemiunnu

This statue of the Great Pyramid architect is held by the Roemer–Pelizaeus Museum in Hildesheim, Germany.

10 Menkaure and his Queen

The Museum of Fine Arts in Boston has a statue of the pyramid builder and his queen.

Suez Canal opening celebration, 1869

TOP 10 Moments in Post-Pharaonic History

1 AD 323: The Christian Era

After the defeat of Cleopatra in 30 BC Egypt became a province of Rome. Following the conversion of Emperor Constantine, Christianity spread throughout the empire and became the official religion in Egypt in AD 323, where its followers were known as Copts. However, due to theological differences, Copts were mercilessly persecuted by the imperial authorities.

Bust of Emperor Constantine

2 640: The Arrival of Islam

Following the teachings of the Prophet Mohammed, the armies of Islam entered Egypt and marched on the fortress of Babylon-in-Egypt near Memphis in AD 640. It surrendered and beside it the Arabs founded the city of Fustat, forerunner of Cairo.

3 969: The Fatimids

Egypt became a province of a vast Islamic empire ruled first from Damascus (by the Umayyad Dynasty), then from Baghdad (by the Abbasid Dynasty). In AD 969 Egypt was seized by the Fatimids from Tunisia. They built a new walled city, which they called Al-Qahira ("The Victorious"), a name later corrupted by European merchants to "Cairo".

4 1250: The Mamluks

Originally slaves brought from the Caucasus to Egypt, the Mamluks accumulated enough power to seize control of Egypt in 1250. Fearsome warriors known for their horsemanship, the Mamluks extended their rule as far north as Turkey. With the spoils of war they endowed Cairo with a legacy of monumental architecture.

5 1516: The Ottomans

From their capital of Constantinople the Ottoman Turks challenged Mamluk power, scoring a decisive victory in 1516. The following year the Ottomans entered Cairo to take control of Egypt.

6 1798: Napoleon's Invasion

In 1798 an army led by Napoleon Bonaparte invaded Egypt and scored a victory in the Battle of the Pyramids. This was short-lived as Napoleon's fleet was subsequently destroyed in the Battle of the Nile by a British Navy led by Admiral Nelson.

Painting depicting the Battle of the Pyramids

Mohammed Ali

7 **1805: Mohammed Ali**
Into the power vacuum left by the French stepped Mohammed Ali, an Albanian mercenary, who defeated forces of Ottomans and Mamluks to seize control of Egypt in 1805. Once in power, he sought to modernize Egypt, promoting industrialization and reform.

8 **1952: Revolution**
The modernization of Egypt resulted in huge debt. In 1882 a revolt was quashed by the British army, who then occupied the country. Resentment against them grew ever stronger, until, in January 1952, "Black Saturday" saw European businesses torched by mobs. On 23 July the Free Officers, led by Gamal Abdel Nasser, seized power in a coup.

9 **1979: Peace with Israel**
Egypt fought Israel in 1948, 1967 and 1973. The first two wars ended in Egyptian defeat, but in 1973 there were military gains, paving the way for peace talks that ended in the signing of the Camp David peace treaty in 1979.

10 **2011–12: Further Revolution**
In January 2011 an uprising swept through Egypt, with protesters demanding an end to political repression, corruption, and the 30-year Mubarak regime. In 2012, Mohamed Morsi of the Muslim Brotherhood won Egypt's first free election.

Top 10 Rulers of Egypt

1 **Amr ibn al-As (c. 583–664)**
The leader of the Islamic army that conquered Egypt.

2 **Salah ad-Din (c. 1138–93)**
Sultan of Egypt and conqueror of Jerusalem, better known in the west as Saladin.

3 **Baybars (1223–77)**
A Mamluk ruler who ended the Crusader presence in the Holy Land.

4 **Suleyman the Great (1494–1566)**
The greatest of Ottoman rulers, whose domains also included Egypt.

5 **Mohammed Ali (1769–1849)**
An Albanian mercenary who founded a ruling dynasty of about 150 years, transforming Egypt from medieval state to modern nation.

6 **Khedive Ismail (1830–95)**
A descendent of Mohammed Ali who built a new, European-style Cairo.

7 **King Farouk (1920–65)**
This puppet king was controlled by the British and sent into exile after the 1952 Revolution *(see p65)*.

8 **Gamal Abdel Nasser (1918–70)**
A socialist president who took on the forces of Britain, France and Israel in the Suez Crisis of 1956, and won *(see p65)*.

9 **Anwar Sadat (1918–81)**
Sadat sued for peace with Israel and was assassinated by Islamic extremists in 1981.

10 **Hosni Mubarak (b.1928)**
Mubarak was in power for 30 years before anti-government protests overthrew him in 2011.

Left **The Mamluk mosque of Sultan Hassan, Cairo** Right **Mashrabiya in Islamic Cairo**

Top 10 Islamic Architecture

1 The Mosque
Egypt's oldest mosque, the Mosque of Amr *(see p84)*, was built in AD 640. Architectural styles developed rapidly under successive early Islamic dynasties to peak under the Mamluks (1250–1516), when craftsmen from all over the Near East were brought to Egypt to build for vainglorious sultans, with often remarkable results that rival Europe's great Gothic cathedrals.

2 Domes and Minarets
One of the greatest achievements of Cairo's medieval artisans was the decorative carving of stone surfaces, seen at its best on the city's myriad minarets and, particularly, its domes. Developed under the Mamluks, the decoration of domes became an increasingly sophisticated art culminating in mesmerizing interwoven patterns of geometric and floral designs.

3 Madrassa
A *madrassa* is a Koranic school, where law and theology are taught. Historically, mosques and *madrassas* have often been housed in the same building. A mosque tends to incorporate teaching rooms or has *iwans* – large arched spaces arranged around a central courtyard, in which lessons are given.

A mihrab with inlaid marble

4 Domestic Architecture
Private houses *(beit)* owed their design to climatic and social conditions. They were inward-looking for privacy, with rooms arranged around a central courtyard. Small windows, large airy rooms, shady arcades, fountains and rooftop "wind catchers" that channelled cool breezes kept the houses cool.

5 Mashrabiya
These are wooden-lattice screens. Long before glass became common, *mashrabiya* was used to cover windows, either externally or internally. The screens allowed the women of the house to observe without themselves being seen.

The carved dome of a mosque

6 Wikala
Also known as a *caravanserai*, this is the forerunner of the modern hotel. From early Islamic times it provided lodgings to the merchant caravans that brought goods to medieval Egypt.

7 Sabil-Kuttab

Public fountains *(sabils)* are a typical element of Islamic architecture – some no more than a tap and a trough, some grand like the Sabil-Kuttab of Abdel Rahman Katkhuda in Cairo *(see p87)*. The *kuttab* was an open loggia or gallery where teachings of the Koran took place.

8 Mausoleum

Just like the pharaohs before them, Egypt's medieval sultans sought to glorify themselves in death by building funerary complexes of mosques and *madrassas* beside a domed tomb chamber. Some of the best examples of these are in Cairo's Northern Cemetery *(see p85)*.

9 Inlaid Marble

Intricate designs using different coloured pieces of marble often decorate the walls or ceilings of Egypt's mosques, *madrassas* and mausoleums, as well as the *mihrab*, the alcove-like niche that indicates the Muslims' direction of prayer.

Brightly painted woodwork in a mosque

10 Woodwork

Wooden ceilings in the prayer halls of mosques were often carved with intricate geometric patterns and painted in rich colours. Doors were also often inlaid with pieces of ivory. Fine examples of this can be seen at the Museum of Islamic Art in Cairo *(see pp46 and 74)*.

Top 10 Islamic Monuments

1 Mosque of Ibn Tulun
It is worth visiting this, one of the oldest mosques in Egypt, for its unique minaret *(see p84)*.

2 Mosque of Al-Azhar
Egypt's most important mosque consists of a catalogue of architectural styles, from the 10th to the 19th century *(see pp14–15)*.

3 Beit al-Suhaymi
There are fine examples of *mashrabiya* in this former merchant's house *(see p87)*.

4 Mosque of Sultan Hassan
The courtyard of this majestic 13th-century mosque served as a *madrassa* with four soaring *iwans (see p85)*.

5 Mosque of Sultan Qaitbey
This mosque in Cairo's Northern Cemetery has a very fine carved stone dome.

6 Gayer-Anderson Museum
This old house boasts impressive *mashrabiya*-screened galleries *(see p46)*.

7 Mosque of Suleyman Pasha
Beautiful inlaid marble and woodwork can be seen in this Ottoman mosque *(see p86)*.

8 Madrassa-Mausoleum of Qalaoun
Qalaoun's great edifice has some fine inlaid marble decoration *(see p87)*.

9 Wikala of Al-Ghouri
This is the most impressive *wikala* in Cairo *(see p15)*.

10 Manial Palace
This 19th-century royal residence built in traditional Islamic style has beautiful painted ceilings *(see p72)*.

Left **Egyptian Museum** Right **Coptic Museum**

TOP 10 Museums

1 Egyptian Museum, Cairo

Egypt's principal museum sits just off Cairo's central square, Midan Tahrir, and beside the Nile. Along with the Pyramids, this is the city's must-see sight. You need to allow at least half a day to see the highlights, which include the treasures of Tutankhamun, mummies of pharaohs and three millennias' worth of statues, but it is really worth returning for a second visit as there is too much to take in at one go *(see pp8–11)*.

2 Gayer-Anderson Museum, Cairo

Abutting the magnificent Ibn Tulun Mosque *(see p84)*, this unusual museum – named for its former owner, British Army officer Major John Gayer-Anderson – is composed of two adjoining 16th-century houses that were refurbished by the major and filled with antiquities, artworks and Oriental artefacts.

Bust of Nefertiti, Gayer-Anderson Museum

The rooms themselves are exquisite and are decorated in a variety of styles, including Turkish, Persian, Damascene and even Chinese. *Map H6 • Sharia Ibn Tulun • 02 2364 7822 • Open 9am–4pm • Adm £E35*

3 Museum of Islamic Art, Cairo

This museum, devoted to 7th–19th-century arts and crafts, holds some stunning exhibits, many of which originate in the mosques and old houses of Cairo's medieval quarters. There are wonderful examples of huge carved doors, etched silverware, mosaic floors and *mashrabiya* (wooden-lattice) screens, as well as old Korans and manuscripts from around the Islamic world. Often overlooked by visitors, this museum is definitely worth seeing *(see p74)*.

4 Coptic Museum, Cairo

Treasures from the 300 years between the end of the worship of pagan gods and the birth of Islam are displayed in this beautiful two-storey museum at the heart of Coptic Cairo. Some exhibits demonstrate the link between the old gods of Egypt and early Christianity, notably the transformation of the ancient Egyptian *ankh* symbol into the cross. There are also finely woven textiles on display, for which the Copts were once famous *(see p84)*.

Funerary slab, Graeco-Roman Museum

5 Graeco-Roman Museum, Alexandria

This revered museum exhibits a fascinating collection relating to the Ptolemaic era – the three centuries spanning around 300–30 BC, from the time of Alexander the Great to Cleopatra. It also has exhibits covering the Roman period up until the Arab conquest in AD 640. Highlights include some superb mosaics and a giant Apis bull in basalt from the time of Hadrian, found at the Serapeum, the site of classical Alexandria's main temple *(see p95)*.

6 Alexandria National Museum

Inaugurated in 2003 and housed in a villa that formerly contained the US Consulate, this museum combines chronologically arranged collections from the Pharaonic, Coptic and Islamic periods. There are also some 19th-century examples of glassware, weaponry and jewellery, as well as a few items of statuary recovered from the seabed in recent times. All exhibits are beautifully presented and well labelled *(see p95)*.

7 Imhotep Museum, Saqqara

Opened in 2006, this museum displays finds from the site of Saqqara. The prize exhibits include a coffin belonging to the architect for whom the museum is named, a painted Graeco-Roman mummy and some green faïence panels from the tomb of Djoser *(see p94)*.

8 Luxor Museum

Although this museum is far smaller than Cairo's Egyptian Museum, the exhibits are better displayed and labelled. Many pieces were discovered locally and mostly date from the New Kingdom era, notably refined statuary, treasures from Tutankhamun's tomb and some fascinating items from the reign of Akhenaten *(see p99)*.

9 Mummification Museum, Luxor

This is a small museum devoted to the subject of death and the afterlife. Exhibits explain the processes of mummification and include tools used for the mummification process. Also displayed are the well-preserved mummy of a 21st-Dynasty high priest of Amun, and a host of mummified animals, as well as some painted coffins *(see p99)*.

Ethnography room, Nubia Museum

10 Nubia Museum, Aswan

The Nubians are a dark-skinned people whose lands have historically straddled the Egyptian–Sudanese border. They have their own distinctive arts and crafts and architecture, as well as a millennia-long history, all of which are celebrated in this purpose-built museum in Aswan *(see p109)*.

Left **Film version of Death on the Nile** Right **Poster for the lavish 1963 film, Cleopatra**

TOP 10 Films Set in Egypt

1 The Spy Who Loved Me
In this 1977 James Bond adventure the requisite foreign exoticism appears in scenes at the Pyramids, Cairo's superb Gayer-Anderson Museum and Karnak. The magnificent temple of Ramses II at Abu Simbel becomes the fictional field headquarters of MI6 containing M's office, conference rooms and Q's laboratory.

2 Ruby Cairo
Largely ignored by cinema audiences, this 1993 film has *Four Weddings and a Funeral* star Andie MacDowell investigating the mystery of her husband's death and enlisting the aid of dashing aid worker Liam Neeson. But the real star is Cairo, where much of the action takes place.

3 Lawrence of Arabia
David Lean's 1962 epic has many scenes that are set in Egypt, which is where the real-life Lawrence worked for a time, at British Army HQ in Cairo. Although all the Egyptian scenes were actually shot in other countries, they look authentic.

4 Cleopatra
As famous for the on-set romance between its two stars, Elizabeth Taylor and Richard Burton, as for the on-screen story, the 1963 "most expensive movie ever made" almost bankrupted 20th Century Fox. It used 79 sets, 26,000 costumes and 1,000 crew members, and Taylor was paid a then record-breaking million-dollar fee.

5 The Mummy
The ancient Egyptian dead can't seem to stay still, judging by the incredible number of mummy movies. The best is still the poignant 1932 original with Boris Karloff in the title role. It was released just a decade after the opening of the tomb of Tutankhamun unleashed the supposed "curse of the pharaoh".

6 The English Patient
Much of the action in the 1996 multi-Oscar-winning film is set in Cairo and Egypt's Western Desert, which was shot in Venice and Tunisia, respectively. The central character of Count Laszlo de Almásy is based on a real character, a Hungarian desert explorer and spy for Germany during World War II.

David Lean's Lawrence of Arabia

For stars of the Egyptian cinema **see pp64–5**

7 The Yacoubian Building
Few Egyptian films ever get an international release, but after being the biggest box office hit of 2006 in Egypt, *The Yacoubian Building* screened around the world. This is a fabulous tale of the intersecting lives of the residents of an apartment block in Downtown Cairo that doubles as a deft and often scathing critique of life in Egypt today.

8 Indiana Jones and the Raiders of the Lost Ark
The first, and best, of the Indiana Jones films, released in 1981, sees the whip-wielding archaeologist on the trail of the Ark of the Covenant, which is discovered at the remains of Tanis, an ancient Egyptian capital in the Delta region of Egypt. However, as often happens, all of the scenes set in Egypt were actually shot in the studio or in Tunisia.

9 Death on the Nile
The 1978 big-screen treatment of Christie's murder mystery didn't stint on the budget, flying cast and crew to Egypt to film at Karnak, Abu Simbel, the Pyramids and the Old Cataract hotel in Aswan. It looks luscious, with an all-star cast headed by Peter Ustinov struggling not to be overshadowed by the scenery.

10 OSS 117: Cairo, Nest of Spies
A hit French comedy that screened worldwide in 2008 featuring OSS 117, a Gallic super-spy, who is a cross between 007 and Austin Powers. Set in 1955, OS 117 is dispatched to Egypt with a simple mission: "Make the Middle East safe." Joyous nonsense ensues.

Top 10 Egypt Must-Reads

1 The Cairo Trilogy
An epic work following the fortunes of a family in 1930s Cairo by Nobel Laureate Naguib Mahfouz *(see p64)*.

2 The Map of Love
Novel by Anglo-Egyptian Ahdaf Soueif, shortlisted for the Booker Prize in 1999.

3 The Cairo House
The fascinating story of a privileged Egyptian family falling foul of the Revolution by Samia Serageldin.

4 A Thousand Miles Up the Nile
Magnificent early travel writing by Amelia Edwards, who in 1873–4 sailed in a dahabiyya from Cairo to Abu Simbel.

5 Egypt: How A Lost Civilization Was Rediscovered
Informative account by Joyce Tyldesley of the development of Egyptology.

6 Moon Tiger
Booker Prize-winning novel by Penelope Lively about a doomed love affair in Egypt during World War II.

7 Taxi
Fictionalized short conversations with Cairo taxi drivers by Khaled al-Khamissi that paint a portrait of Egypt.

8 The Yacoubian Building
Alaa Al-Aswany's massive international bestseller and a movie blockbuster *(see left)*.

9 The Arabian Nightmare
Bizarre fantasy set in the Cairo of the Mamluks by British author Robert Irwin.

10 Death on the Nile
Agatha Christie's best-known murder mystery.

Left **Windsor Hotel, Cairo** Right **Cecil Hotel, Alexandria**

TOP 10 Historic Hotels

1 Shepheard's Hotel, Cairo
Shepheard's of Cairo was once the world's most famous hotel. Founded in 1841, it was famed for its terrace, which overlooked one of the city's busiest streets, and a clientele that ranged from royalty to Noël Coward and Lawrence of Arabia. It was burnt down in the riots of the Egyptian Revolution in 1952 and is commemorated by a plaque at the new Shepheard Hotel built in 1957 on the Corniche. *Map E4 • Corniche al-Nil, Cairo • 020 2792 1000 • www.shepheard-hotel.com*

2 Cairo Marriott
In 1869, when the French Empress Eugénie visited Egypt for the opening of the Suez Canal, she was accommodated in a specially constructed palace set among extensive gardens. This later became a hotel, then in turn a hospital, the headquarters of a government department and the residence of a Levantine magnate. It is now an elegant Marriott hotel *(see p125)*.

Cairo Marriott

3 Windsor Hotel, Cairo
Built in the early 20th century, this has previously been a royal bathhouse and British officers' club. As a hotel it passed into the hands of the current owners in the 1950s and not a thing has been changed since – furniture and fittings all remain the same, including what is believed to be the oldest working lift in Egypt *(see p127)*.

4 Cosmopolitan, Cairo
This fine old Art Nouveau hotel is on a backstreet in central Cairo with a lovely entranceway with original tiling and a revolving wooden door. The lobby boasts stained glass and an old open lift. There are original wooden floors, dark wood furniture and curving balconies, but the rooms are a little unloved. The prices are relatively cheap *(see p126)*.

5 Mena House Oberoi, Giza
A former royal hunting lodge at the Pyramids was transformed into a hotel by an English couple in 1869. In its time it has hosted every emperor, king and president who has visited Egypt. Franklin Roosevelt, Winston Churchill and Chiang Kai-Shek hammered out the final plans for victory over Germany here during World War II *(see p125)*.

Preceding pages **Interior view of the Tomb of Sennefer, Tombs of the Nobles, Luxor**

6 Cecil Hotel, Alexandria

Occupying a prime position on Alexandria's seafront with sweeping views of the harbour, the Cecil was built in 1929. Author Somerset Maugham stayed here, as did Winston Churchill and Chicago gangster Al Capone. The British Secret Service kept a suite here for their operations in World War II and the hotel was immortalized in Lawrence Durrell's novels *The Alexandria Quartet* *(see p128)*.

7 Metropole, Alexandria

Across the square from the Cecil, the Metropole also boasts a great location and is of a similar vintage. Downstairs is the fine 1920s Trianon Café, with high ceilings, original painted wall frescoes and a still popular patisserie section *(see p128)*.

8 Al-Salamlek, Alexandria

At the extreme east of Alexandria in Montazah is a former royal summer residence constructed in a Florentine style and set in beautiful grounds by the sea. A modest outbuilding, known as the Salamlek, has been converted into a luxury hotel, with rooms opulently furnished in stylish period fashion *(see p128)*.

Winter Palace, Luxor

9 Winter Palace, Luxor

Built in 1886 on a prime site fronting the Nile and facing the Theban Hills of the West Bank, the Winter Palace's heyday was in 1922 when the world's media flocked to Luxor in the wake of the discovery of Tutankhamun's tomb. The hotel had to put up tents in the garden to meet the demand for beds *(see p129)*.

10 Old Cataract, Aswan

Built in 1899, the Old Cataract sits on a granite bluff overlooking a rocky stretch of the Nile – the cataract for which the hotel is named. It's a spectacular view, enjoyed by writer Agatha Christie, who stayed here on more than one occasion *(see p131)*.

Old Cataract, Aswan

Vote for your favourite hotel on **traveldk.com**

Left **A glittering array of jewellery** Right **Colourful spices**

Top 10 Souvenirs

1 Papyrus
The papyrus sold throughout Egypt is actually dried banana leaf, printed with designs copied from ancient Egyptian tomb and temple paintings. It costs only a few Egyptian pounds. Real hand-painted papyrus is sold only at specialist galleries such as Dr Ragab's Papyrus Institute in Cairo *(see p55)*.

2 Perfume
Egypt produces many of the essences used by international perfumiers. Undiluted essence can be bought by the ounce in Cairo's Khan al-Khalili souq. Here shops duplicate famous fragrances on request or sell cheap imitations. You can also buy essential oils such as rose or jasmine.

3 Brass and Copperware
The souqs are full of stalls piled high with items made locally, from brass candlesticks and coffee sets to huge wagon wheel-sized copper trays and crescent moons for the tops of minarets. Prices are very cheap, although the quality does vary.

4 Sheesha Pipes
Every Egyptian coffee house is filled with men smoking *sheesha* pipes, the Middle Eastern waterpipe. You'll find them in any souq, but the greatest selection is found in Cairo's Khan al-Khalili *(see p83)*.

Sheesha pipe

5 Egyptian Cotton
Cotton as a crop was introduced into Egypt in the 19th century and almost ever since Egypt has been renowned for the quality of its cotton goods, especially sheets and towels. Much of the best cotton is exported and what you find locally is often inferior. However, certain shops at the malls and hotels sell top-quality goods.

6 Jewellery
Egyptians buy large quantities of gold and silver as traditionally many feel it's safer than putting their money in the banks. Precious metals are sold by the gram in the souqs; with jewellery a percentage is then added to the price for the workmanship. A favourite souvenir is a cartouche with hieroglyphs.

7 Carpets and Rugs
Unlike Turkey, Morocco or Iran, Egypt is not a major carpet-making nation and the work is generally inferior to that in those

Beautifully patterned inlaid boxes

For tips on shopping **see p122**

Alabaster trinkets and brass and copperware

countries. Rugs and tapestries are woven from coarse wool or camel hair, typically in beige and brown. Colourful picture rugs depicting rural scenes are produced at the Ramses Wissa Wassef Art Centre *(see right)*.

8 Spices

Spices are widely sold in the *souqs*. They are fresher and of better quality than the packaged variety sold in the West, especially cinnamon, cumin and *dukkah*, which is a blend of spices.

9 Pharaonic Memorabilia

The sheer number of kitsch Pharaonic souvenirs is overwhelming: alabaster pyramids, plastic replicas of Tutankhamun's death mask, Nefertiti dresses and many others. It is possible to find some attractive small-scale reproductions of ancient Egyptian statuary, and the tiny blue-painted scarabs are fun.

10 Inlay Work

Among the most attractive items produced in Egypt are wooden boxes inlaid with slivers of bone, ivory or mother-of-pearl. Hardwood backgammon boards are also often inlaid in this way.

Top 10 Places to Shop

1 Khan al-Khalili

Cairo's main *souq*, but not a place to go if you like to browse in peace *(see p82)*.

2 Dr Ragab's Papyrus Institute

Art gallery in Cairo that sells some of the best hand-painted papyrus in Egypt. *Map D6 • Corniche al-Nil, Giza, Cairo*

3 First Residence Mall

An opulent mall for the best shopping in Cairo. *Map K2 • 35 Sharia al-Giza, Giza, Cairo*

4 Tentmakers' Souq

Cairo's only remaining covered market where you can find beautiful handcrafted appliqué work. *Map H4 • Sharia al-Muizz li-Din Allah, Cairo*

5 Zamalek

A district of Cairo home to several good jewellery and homeware boutiques *(see p72)*.

6 Ramses Wissa Wassef Art Centre

The handwoven, beautifully crafted tapestries for sale here are unique works of art. *Map B2 • Harrania Village, Saqqara Road, Al-Haram, Giza*

7 Attarine

A district in central Alexandria renowned for its antique shops – just don't expect any bargains. *Map S2*

8 Aswan Souq

The best *souq* in Egypt outside Cairo, especially for spices *(see p108)*.

9 At the Hotel

Prices are marked up but quality is generally assured at shops at the better hotels.

10 Onboard Your Cruise Ship

Most cruise ships have a small shop onboard with a cross-section of local goods.

For more on shopping in Cairo **see p76**

Left **Al-Azhar Park** Right **Aquarium in the Fish Gardens**

TOP 10 Children's Attractions in Cairo

1 Egyptian Museum

Children of all ages enjoy this museum. Besides the Tutankhamun treasures, which are always popular, children find the Mummy Room fascinating, and in particular the collection of animal mummies that include bandaged cats, monkeys and even a crocodile. Youngsters also enjoy the large collection of Middle Kingdom models on the first floor, which may look like toys but were believed by the ancient Egyptians to come to life in the afterlife *(see pp8–11)*.

2 Giza Zoo

The zoo was founded in 1891 and has a central feature of twin hills connected by a bridge designed by Gustave Eiffel. A maze of pathways loops around animal enclosures and it's possible to take part in feeding sessions. Avoid Fridays when it gets overcrowded. The First Residence Mall across the road has a café with good ice creams. *Map K3 • Sharia al-Giza, Giza, Cairo • Open 8:30am–5:30pm • Adm*

A goat in Giza Zoo

3 Fish Gardens

Officially known as the Gabalaya Gardens, this is a small public park on the island of Zamalek, adorned with tall palm trees and grassy hillocks. The hillocks cover cave-like rooms that contain large aquariums with fish and turtles. *Map D2 • Sharia Geziret al-Wusta, Zamalek, Cairo • Open 8:30am–4:40pm • Adm*

4 Al-Azhar Park

A well-tended modern park on the eastern edge of the city, Al-Azhar is very popular with families and children, thanks to its wide-open spaces, grassy hills and ornamental lake. There is an excellent children's play area, which includes climbing frames, walkways and swings, as well as cafés and snack shops. *Map J4–5 • Sharia Salah Salem, Cairo • 02 2510 3868 and 19135 • Open 9am–2am in summer, 9am–midnight in winter • www.alazharpark.com • Adm*

5 Felucca Rides

Feluccas – the small boats with triangular-shaped sails – can be hired by the hour from landings just in front of the Shepheard's Hotel and the Four Seasons Nile Plaza *(see p125)*. They seat eight people and cost about £E80 per hour plus £E10 tip, although this is negotiable. Pack a picnic and eat out on the river while watching the sun go down over the city. If the kids dip their hands in the water, make sure they wash them afterwards.

An acrobat at the National Circus

6 National Circus

Housed in a purpose-built structure beside the Nile, the circus operates year round. All the performers are Egyptian and include jugglers, acrobats, tightrope walkers, lion- and tiger-tamers, magicians and trained dogs. The show lasts just over two hours. ⊗ *Map H1 • Sharia al-Nil, Agouza, Cairo • Shows daily (except Wed) at 9pm (one hour earlier in winter) • Adm*

7 Diwan Bookshop

Cairo's best bookshop has a small but excellent dedicated children's section with books for all ages in both English and Arabic. Look out for titles that are set in Egypt such as the beautifully illustrated *The Day of Ahmed's Secret*. The story follows Ahmed through the streets of Cairo as he delivers butane gas to customers *(see p75)*.

8 The Pyramids of Giza

Many children are just as spellbound by the Pyramids as adults. The opportunity to go inside some pyramids and descend the passageways to the buried chambers is particularly exciting, as well as the horse and camel rides *(see pp12–13)*.

9 Dr Ragab's Pharaonic Village

This educational theme park recreates life in ancient Egypt using about 100 actors. Board a boat for a tour that includes visits to ancient houses, a temple and a walk-through replica of Tutankhamun's tomb complete with treasure. Children can have their photograph taken in Pharaonic costume. There are also several museums, as well as a bazaar, playground and cafeteria. ⊗ *Map K6 • 3 Sharia Bahr al-Azam, Giza, Cairo • 02 3568 8601 • Open 9am–9pm in summer, 9am–6pm in winter • www.pharaonicvillage.com • Adm (children under 4 yrs free)*

10 Dream Park

Egypt's largest amusement park is a 30-minute car journey from central Cairo. It contains a large variety of fairground rides, including a roller coaster, a log flume ride, go-karts and bumper cars. In addition, it has the usual videogame arcades and themed restaurant areas. ⊗ *Map H1 • Al-Wahat Road, 6th October City, 20 km (12 miles) SW of central Cairo • 02 3855 3191 • Open 4pm–midnight daily (from noon Fri) • www.dreamparkegypt.com • Adm*

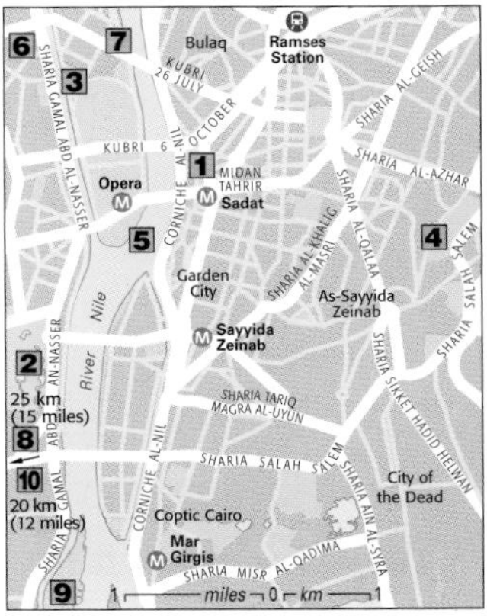

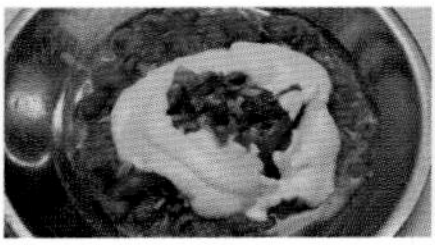

Left **Fuul** Centre **Taamiya** Right **Mahalabiya**

Top 10 Egyptian Dishes

1 Fuul
The most popular streetfood snack in Egypt, *fuul* is a paste of mashed broad (fava) beans flavoured with garlic and olive oil. It is ladelled out of large copper pots, often into pockets of pitta bread and typically sold as an inexpensive takeaway sandwich.

2 Taamiya
Another Egyptian streetfood staple, known elsewhere as falafel, *taamiya* is made with mashed fava beans and parsley (instead of chickpeas, which are used elsewhere around the Mediterranean). It is made in the shape of flat discs rather than round balls and is typically eaten as a sandwich with salad.

3 Koshari
A mix of rice, brown lentils and macaroni topped with fried onions and a spicy tomato sauce, *koshari* is normally eaten in dedicated *koshari* restaurants that serve the dish exclusively.

Koshari

Creatively presented kofta and lamb kebabs

4 Shawarma
Like the Turkish doner kebab, *shawarma* is a large cone of pressed lamb or chicken that is rotated vertically in front of a flame grill. As the meat is cooked it is sliced off and mixed on a griddle with chopped tomato, onion and parsley before being rolled in a large disc of flatbread and wrapped in foil to take away.

5 Kofta and Kebab
Flame-grilled chunks of lamb (kebab) and spiced minced meat made into a sausage and grilled on a skewer *(kofta)* are a favourite Egyptian meal. It is typically eaten with a simple chopped tomato and cucumber salad and a disc of flatbread.

6 Molokhiya
Hard to like on first encounter, this is a soup made from mallow leaves. Green in colour, it has a thick, viscous texture. Egyptians eat it with meat such as rabbit or lamb. Fatimid Sultan Hakim found the dish so unappetizing that he had it banned in the 11th century.

7 Pigeon

A traditional delicacy, pigeons *(hamaam)* are bred throughout Egypt in conical pigeon towers. They are stuffed with seasoned rice or, even better, bulgur wheat *(freek)* before being grilled or baked.

8 Desserts

Egyptian desserts are quite light. *Mahalabiya* is a delicate rosewater-flavoured ground rice dessert, topped with toasted nuts and cinnamon. *Um Ali* is similar to the English bread and butter pudding but is less soft and spongy as it is made with local dry breads. *Roz bi laban* is rice pudding, which is always served cold.

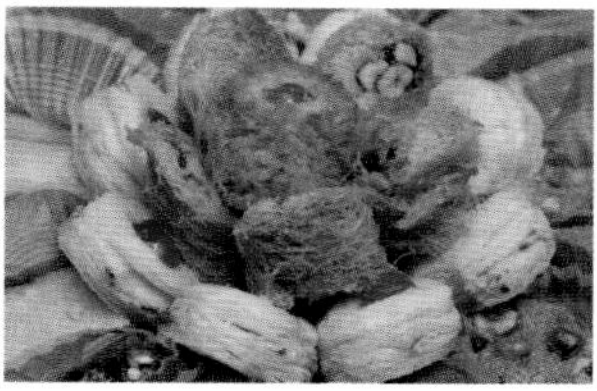

A selection of baklava

9 Baklava

Egyptians are big fans of the sticky, syrup-drenched, nut-filled filo pastries known collectively as *baklava*. There are numerous different kinds such as *konafa*, which has a cream base and a crunchy vermicelli pastry crust and *basbousa*, made of semolina pastry soaked in honey and topped with hazelnuts.

10 Fiteer

Fiteer is a light, flaky multi-layered bread made from dough stretched paper thin and folded several times. It is served stuffed with minced meat or cheese or just plain, brushed with *samneh* (ghee) or dusted with icing sugar.

Top 10 Egyptian Drinks

1 Limoon

A refreshing summer drink of squeezed lemon juice, water and sugar, served with ice.

2 Sahlab

A winter drink made from the starch in the ground bulb of an orchid, mixed with milk, sugar and rosewater, then garnished with chopped pistachios and cinnamon.

3 Karkade

A drink that can be served either hot or cold, made from the boiled, dried leaves of the hibiscus plant, with sugar added to taste.

4 Yansoon

An anise tea said to be effective against colds.

5 Fresh Fruit Juices

Juice stalls are common throughout Egypt, serving juices from pomegranate or orange to guava or mango.

6 Sugarcane Juice

Even more popular (it's cheaper) than fruit juice is sugarcane juice *(asab)*. The cane is ground up and served as a milky green liquid.

7 Tea

Tea *(shai)* is served strong and extremely sweet. For Western-style tea ask for "shai lipton", made with a teabag.

8 Coffee

Traditional *qahwa* (coffee) is a Turkish-style coffee, served sweet. For Western coffee ask for "nescaf".

9 Stella

Local Egyptian beer, a low-strength lager, is called Stella.

10 Mineral Water

Drinking bottled water is recommended. Available throughout the country, a 1.5-litre bottle costs £E3–5.

Left **Felfela, Cairo** Right **White & Blue, Alexandria**

Top 10 Restaurants

1 Abu al-Sid, Cairo

It is often said that Egyptian cooking is a domestic cuisine, not especially suited to a high-class restaurant. Abu al-Sid proves otherwise. This is a very fashionable restaurant, decorated in an Oriental style with hanging lamps and brass tables, which has single-handedly made dining out on traditional delicacies fashionable. Specialities include stuffed pigeon and *molokhiya* with rabbit *(see p79)*.

Aqua at the Four Seasons Nile Plaza, Cairo

2 Aqua at the Four Seasons Nile Plaza, Cairo

Much of the best dining in Egypt is at the many five-star hotels. Those that stand out are the Four Seasons establishments, particularly Cairo's Four Seasons at the Nile Plaza *(see p125)*, which boasts five excellent dining options, including Aqua, a superb seafood restaurant with splendid views of the Nile and an excellent sushi bar. At the entrance there is an impressive aquarium with exotic, brightly-coloured fish *(see p79)*.

3 Buddha Bar, Cairo

Sumptuous, striking and hip, Buddha Bar sets the standard for cool in Cairo. The split-level restaurant is presided over by a giant smiling Buddha, while the impressive outdoor terrace offers stunning Nile views. Asian fusion food and the best sushi in town are on the menu, and a dazzling cocktail list aids the transition from dining to dancing. The Buddha's signature ambient music gives way to live DJs later in the evening *(see p79)*.

4 Felfela, Cairo

A long-standing favourite with tourists as well as locals, Felfela specializes in inexpensive Egyptian street fare served in fun surroundings consisting of tree-trunk tables, aquariums of tropical fish and terrapins, and twittering birds in cages. This is the perfect restaurant to sample traditional staples such as *fuul*, *taamiya* and grilled pigeon. Try the *hosniya*, which is *fuul* with egg and cream baked in the oven *(see p79)*.

5 Osmanly at the Kempinski Nile Hotel, Cairo

This Turkish restaurant features a menu that's both innovative and authentic. It's a welcoming, modestly sized, uncluttered space perfect for a leisurely feast. The wine cellar is well stocked and, uniquely in Cairo, all foreign wines can be ordered by the glass *(see pp79 & 125)*.

For information on Egyptian dishes see **pp58–9**

1886 Restaurant, Winter Palace, Luxor

6 La Bodega, Cairo

Housed on the first floor of a *belle époque* apartment block with high-ceilinged rooms, the Bodega is a stylish restaurant, bar and cocktail lounge popular with Cairo's city slickers. Its Aperitivo bar serves superb Italian cuisine, while Bistro's menu offers well-prepared and impeccably fresh Mediterranean and French dishes *(see p79)*.

7 White & Blue, Alexandria

Alexandria is renowned for its many fine fish restaurants, but what makes this restaurant particularly special is its location, elevated above a small beach and overlooking the fishing fleet gathered in the harbour. The fare is simple but very fresh and satisfying. Guests choose their own fish from a chiller cabinet and wait while it's fried, baked or grilled. The entrance to the restaurant is just opposite Fort Qaitbey. *Map S1 • Greek Club, Sharia Bahary • 03 480 2690 • ££££*

8 Al-Borg, Port Said

Al-Borg is a simple family restaurant on the beach that prepares only the freshest seafood, including a great local variation on bouillabaisse. The portions are huge and prices are reasonable. *Map B1 • Sharia Tahr al-Bahr, Al-Arab • 066 332 3442 • Closed dinner • ££££*

9 1886 Restaurant at the Winter Palace, Luxor

For all its many other attractions, the restaurants in Luxor are rarely particularly memorable. The exception is in the dining room of the grand Winter Palace hotel, where French classic dishes are served in elegant old-world surroundings. Watch the sun go down behind the Valley of the Kings on the Nile-facing front terrace before dinner. Formal dress must be worn *(see pp53 & 106)*.

10 1902 Restaurant at the Old Cataract, Aswan

Like its near-neighbour Luxor, Aswan offers few treats for gourmets. Food is basic café fare in most establishments. The exception is the signature restaurant at the venerable Old Cataract hotel. Here the menu is comprised of gourmet nouvelle cuisine and local fish specialities. Best of all is the dining hall itself – a sumptuous Moorish fantasy with red and white arches and fine *mashrabiya* *(see pp53 & 131)*.

1902 Restaurant at the Old Cataract, Aswan

For a key to price categories see **pp79 & 89**

Left **Pharaons' Rally** Right **The sun illuminating the statue of Ramses II at Abu Simbel**

Top 10 Festivals and Events

1 Ramadan

Ramadan is the Islamic month of fasting. During daylight hours observant Muslims must not eat, drink or smoke. The fast is broken at sunset with *iftar* (breakfast), a meal usually enjoyed with all the family. Although tempers can be frayed during the day (especially when Ramadan falls during summer heat), it is a festive time with many people out on the streets until the early hours of the morning. The celebrations peak with Eid al-Fitr, a three-day feast to mark Ramadan's end.

2 Sun Festival of Ramses II

On 22 February and 22 October every year, the sun penetrates 55 m (180 ft) into the innermost chamber of the Sun Temple of Ramses II at Abu Simbel. It illuminates three of the quartet of statues of seated gods that lie deep in the innermost chamber *(see p31)*.

3 Pharaons' Rally

Taking place every September/October, this is a gruelling week-long, 2,800-km (1,700-mile) motor vehicle race (including cars, trucks and motor bikes) through the Egyptian desert, with the Pyramids as both starting and finishing point. People come from all over the world to compete. *www.pharaonsrally.com*

4 Cairo International Film Festival

An often chaotic celebration of local and international film takes place in November/December every year in various cinemas across the capital. It is usually attended by a bevy of Arab world and international film stars. The festival is hugely popular with local Egyptians because the festival screenings' censorship laws are relaxed and international films are screened uncut. *www.cairofilmfest.org*

Worshippers praying during Ramadan at the Al-Azhar Mosque, Cairo

Celebrations of the Prophet's Birthday

5 The Prophet's Birthday

Also known as the Moulid an-Nabi, this major holiday celebrates the birth of the Prophet Mohammed. The streets burst into colour and noise. Like all Islamic holy days, it follows the Islamic calendar, which is about 11 days shorter than the Western calendar. As a result, Islamic holidays move forward every year compared with the Western calendar.

6 Moulid of Al-Hussein

A *moulid* is a saint-worshipping festival taking the form of riotous street parties, complete with chanting, dancing, music, fairground rides and sideshows. It lasts several days, culminating in the *Leyla Kebira*, meaning "Big Night". One of the largest is focused on the Mosque of Al-Hussein in Islamic Cairo.

7 Eid al-Adha

This is a commemoration of Abraham's willingness to sacrifice his son as an act of obedience to God. During the two-day holiday Muslims slaughter a sheep or goat and distribute the meat among the poor. It is also a time for visiting family and friends, and for exchanging gifts.

8 Moulid of Abu al-Haggag

This festival honours Luxor's patron saint, whose mosque sits on top of Luxor Temple *(see p21)*. Giant floats travel through the densely packed streets, and there is drumming, ritualistic stick fights and horse races. The *moulid* occurs the month before Ramadan and so the date changes each year.

9 Cairo International Book Fair

Taking place every January or February, the biggest cultural event on the Egyptian calendar attracts publishers, authors and buyers from all over the world. Crowds turn up for a programme of talks, reading, debates and lectures, and for the many stalls selling everything from DVDs to streetfood. *www.cairobookfair.org*

10 Egyptian Marathon

Every January or February, when it is as cool as it ever gets in Upper Egypt, this marathon is held on the West Bank at Luxor. The start and finishing point is the Temple of Hatshepsut. *www.egyptianmarathon.com*

Competitors at the Egyptian Marathon

Left **King Farouk** Right **Fifi Abdou**

TOP 10 Icons of Popular Culture

1 Umm Kulsum

It is impossible to overstate the significance of Umm Kulsum, the Arab world's greatest ever singer. Until she retired in 1972, she was the voice of the nation for more than 30 years, and when she died in 1975 her funeral in Cairo drew two million mourners out onto the streets.

2 Fifi Abdou

This much loved national icon is renowned for her cheeky and earthy belly dancing routines. Now too old to dance, Abdou has forged a successful career as a TV and film actress, usually playing the role of a "woman of the people".

3 Naguib Mahfouz

Arguably the greatest 20th-century writer of the Arab world, Mahfouz (1911–2006) was a life-long civil servant who nevertheless produced more than 30 novels as well as many short stories and plays. In 1988 he became the first and only Arab to win the Nobel Prize for Literature.

Naguib Mahfouz

4 Abdel Halim Hafez

Dubbed the "Dark Nightingale", Hafez (1929–77), was one of the most popular Egyptian singers and actors not only in Egypt but throughout the Middle East from the 1950s to the 1970s. Like Um Kolsum, his music is still played on the radio daily.

5 Adel Imam

Possibly Egypt's most popular film and stage actor, Imam has been a star on screen since the early 1960s. He has appeared in more than 100 films, primarily as a comedian. He continues to enjoy box-office success and often secures major roles in TV dramas.

6 Egypt's Awakening

Mahmoud Mokhtar (1891–1934) is considered the father of modern Egyptian sculpture. His most iconic work, *Egypt's Awakening*, which depicts a peasant woman lifting her veil with one hand as she rests the other on a sphinx, stands near Cairo University in Giza.

7 Gamal Abdel Nasser

Following Egypt's Revolution in 1952 *(see p43)*, Nasser (1918–70) became a figurehead not just for Egypt and the Arab World, but for many African nations struggling to emerge from decades of colonial rule. Although his policies and achievements are now subject to debate, he remains, nearly 40 years after his death, adored by millions.

Gamal Abdel Nasser

8 The Pyramids
The pyramids are the most recognizable symbols of Egypt and, if a controversial law is passed, they will be confined to Egypt. Since 2008 officials have been working to make it illegal to produce replicas or sell images of the Pyramids outside Egypt.

9 Omar Sharif
Possibly the only Egyptian other than Tutankhamun whose face is instantly recognized around the world, thanks to roles in major films such as *Lawrence of Arabia* (1962) and *Doctor Zhivago* (1965), Sharif is back in Cairo appearing on TV and making Arabic- and French-language films.

10 King Farouk
Crowned in 1937, Farouk (1920–65) was the last proper king of Egypt. His reign was brought to an end by the 1952 Revolution. He has remained a subject of fascination for his marriages, his lavish lifestyle and corrupt regime.

Top 10 International Pyramids

1 The Louvre Pyramid, Paris
Architect IM Pei's startling 1989 reworked entrance to France's major museum.

2 The Luxor, Las Vegas
A luxury hotel and casino in the form of a vast black pyramid, opened in 1993.

3 Raffles, Dubai
A pyramid-shaped hotel, linked to an ancient Egypt-themed shopping mall.

4 The New Great Pyramid, Dessau
Not yet built, a huge pyramid that will house the cremated remains of millions in Germany.

5 Transamerica Pyramid, San Francisco
A landmark 1970s skyscraper in the form of an elongated 48-storey pyramid.

6 The Bosnian Pyramid, Visoko
Not a pyramid apparently but "a cruel hoax on an unsuspecting public" according to debunkers.

7 The Great American Pyramid, Memphis, Tennessee
A multi-purpose arena modelled on the Great Pyramid at Giza.

8 The Gympie Pyramid, Queensland, Australia
Built by ancient Egyptians, Incas or Italian immigrants – the debate rages on!

9 Ryugyong Hotel, Pyongyang
A 105-storey pyramidal hotel in North Korea, labelled "The Worst Building in the History of Mankind".

10 Funerary Pyramids
Fashionable in the 18th–19th centuries, one of the finest pyramid mausoleums is at Blickling Park, Norfolk, England.

Left **Cairo Opera House** Centre **A belly dancer entertains** Right **A cinema film poster**

Top 10 Entertainment

1 Coffee Houses

Egypt's traditional coffee houses *(qahwa)* are a million miles from Starbucks. The coffee comes in just two varieties – with sugar and without – and is secondary to socializing, watching football, playing backgammon and smoking *sheesha* pipes. They are the equivalent of the English pub or French corner café.

2 Cinema

Egyptian cinema is the Hollywood of the Arab world, producing hundreds of films each year. Egypt's many cinemas tend mostly to show local films, but the multi-screen venues in the modern malls also show subtitled imports.

3 Belly Dancing

Many hotels in Egypt have a nightclub at which belly dancers perform. Pyramids Road (Sharia al-Ahram), which runs from Giza to the Pyramids, also has several nightclubs featuring belly dancing.

4 Bars

Islam prohibits alcohol, but the choice of whether to observe this prohibition is left to the individual. Beer and wine are served in many restaurants, and major cities have bars although they tend to be hidden away from the public gaze. Any tourist hotel will also have a bar.

5 Arabic Music

Cairo's Opera House *(see p75)* and Alexandria's Sayed Darwish Theatre stage many live performances of Arabic classical music. In Islamic Cairo, particularly during Ramadan, there are often music evenings at the Beit Zeinab Khatoun and Beit al-Suhaymi *(see pp14–15 & 87)*.

6 Spectator Sports

Football reigns supreme in Egypt. Top teams in the domestic leagues are Zamalek and Al-Ahly, both in Cairo. Games are played on Fridays and watched in coffee houses throughout Egypt.

A captivating performance by whirling dervishes

A traditional coffee house

7 Folkloric Performances

The most unusual and compelling folkloric performance is given by the Whirling Dervishes, who can be seen at the Wikala al-Ghouri in Cairo *(see p77)*. Some hotels in Luxor and Aswan put on folkloric shows.

8 Rock, Pop and Jazz

Al-Sawy Culture Wheel in Cairo has live music several times a week by young, local bands, and the Cairo Jazz Club hosts regular live jazz *(see p75)*. Foreign cultural centres such as the British Council and the Alliance Française sometimes sponsor gigs, details of which can be found in the local press.

9 Art Galleries

There's a vibrant local art scene in Cairo, with up to a dozen small galleries hosting regularly changing and well attended exhibitions. The best of the galleries are Downtown and in Zamalek *(see p75)*.

10 Sound and Light Shows

Every major site in Egypt presents a sound and light show once the sun goes down. The monument is illuminated by coloured floodlights while a recorded voice narrates snippets of history and mythology. The narration often leaves something to be desired but it's worth revisiting the sites by moonlight.

Top 10 Egyptian Playlist

1. **Umm Kulsum *Inta Omri***
A 45-minute track by the Arab world's greatest ever singer *(see p64)*.

2. **Abdel Halim Hafez *Banat al-Yom***
A soundtrack to old black and white movies starring Egypt's beloved crooner *(see p64)*.

3. **Amr Diab *Best Of***
The brightest Egyptian pop talent of the last 20 years.

4. **Ruby *Meshit Wara Ehsasy***
Second album by the much talked about young singer, thanks to her provocative lyrics and videos.

5. **Mohammed Mounir *Taam al-Bayoot***
Album by a ground-breaking singer, who combines Arabic pop with his Nubian roots.

6. **Hakim *Yaho***
Arabic *shaabi* (street-pop) that launched the singer on an international career.

7. **Ahmed Adaweyah *Zaqma***
One of the pioneers of the *shaabi* sound, renowned for mixing pop with social commentary: the title of this album means "crowded".

8. **Ali Hassan Kuban *Walk Like a Nubian***
Nubian music isn't listened to much in Egypt but Kuban (who died in 2001) enjoys a big international following.

9. **Shaban Abdel Rahim *Ana Bakrah Israel***
A former dry cleaner whose political lyrics made him a huge star in the late 1990s.

10. **Warda *Batwanese Beek***
A hugely loved and respected grande dame of the pop scene.

AROUND CAIRO & THE NILE

Left **View of Cairo Opera House from Rhoda Island** Right **Detail of the façade of the Manial Palace**

Central Cairo

UNTIL THE MIDDLE OF THE 19TH CENTURY *Cairo was a walled medieval city, with a street plan largely unaltered since the time of the Fatimids* (see p42). *This changed with the rule of Khedive Ismail (1863–79), who had been educated in France and wanted to reshape his capital into a modern and smart city similar to Paris. Rather than try to impose order on the existing city, he created an entirely new city with tree-lined boulevards, squares and fine European architecture on the flood plain between the medieval walls and the Nile. This remains the heart of central Cairo and is, for the most part, compact enough to explore on foot. Since then the city has crossed the Nile to the west bank and spread all the way to the foot of the Pyramids, as well as extending far to the north and the south in a series of modern suburbs.*

TOP 10 Sights

1. **Egyptian Museum**
2. **Downtown**
3. **Cairo Opera House Complex**
4. **Cairo Tower**
5. **Zamalek**
6. **Manial Palace**
7. **Bulaq**
8. **Mahmoud Khalil Museum**
9. **The Nile**
10. **The Pyramids**

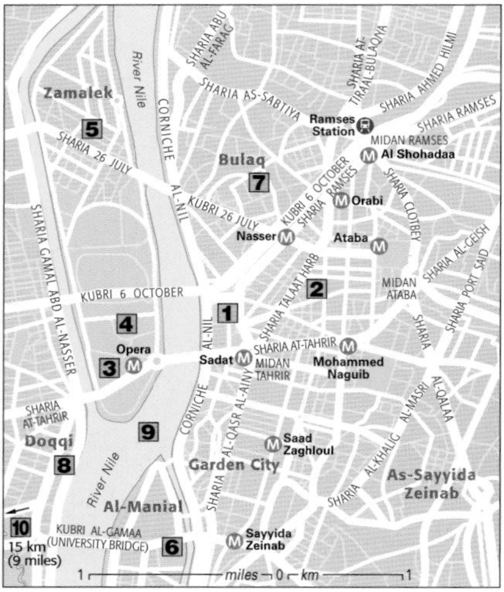

Cairo Tower

Preceding pages **Detail of columns of the temple at Kom Ombo, near Aswan**

1 Egyptian Museum

Right at the heart of the modern city, on Midan Tahrir (Cairo's main, traffic-choked square), is the country's main museum. It's one of the top museums in the world, thanks to an unequalled collection of artefacts from ancient Egypt, ranging from small pieces of delicate jewellery to towering colossi of the pharaohs and the Tutankhamun Galleries. It is advisable to arrive early to avoid the crowds and to allow as much time as possible to see the exhibits *(see pp8–11)*.

A statue in front of the Egyptian Museum

2 Downtown

This is the 19th-century city created by Ismail. It stretches east of the Egyptian Museum and is centred on two main intersecting streets: Sharia Talaat Harb and Sharia Qasr al-Nil. Both are busy shopping streets, lined with storefronts displaying gaudy clothing and shoes. Some of the architecture *(see p73,* Walk in "Paris on the Nile"*)* is beautiful, much of it in an Italianate style, but it is very dilapidated as in recent times all investment and growth has been concentrated in the suburbs.

Midan Talaat Harb, Downtown

3 Cairo Opera House Complex

Cairo's original opera house was built in 1869 for the opening of the Suez Canal and was located Downtown on what is still known as Midan Opera. It burnt to the ground in 1971 and it was only in 1988 that the city finally got its new opera house, a stunning, modernist update on Islamic architecture, designed and funded by the Japanese. It sits in beautifully landscaped grounds, which also house the impressive Museum of Modern Egyptian Art *(see p75)*. ✎ *Map D–E4*

• Opera House: Sharia at-Tahrir, Gezira, 02 2739 0144, www.cairoopera.org

• Museum of Modern Art: Cairo Opera House Grounds, Gezira, 02 2736 6667, open 9am–2pm, 5–9pm Tue–Sun, Adm

4 Cairo Tower

For the best city views, visit this 1962 tower on the island of Gezira, where a lift takes you 185 m (610 ft) up to a viewing platform. The panorama stretches from the cliffs of the Muqattam Hills, which constrain the city's spread to the east, all the way west to the Pyramids, which mark the point at which Cairo meets the desert. The best time to go up the tower is at sunset, when millions of lights twinkle into life and the evening call to prayer sounds out below from a thousand or more mosques. ✎ *Map E4*

• Sharia Hadayek al-Zuhreya, Gezira • 02 2736 5112 • Open 8am–midnight • Adm

5 Zamalek

The island in the middle of the Nile, just across from central Cairo, is known as Gezira (which is the Arabic word for "island"). Occupying its northern half is the smart neighbourhood of Zamalek. It has always been an enclave enjoyed by privileged European residents and wealthy Egyptian families. The main street, Sharia 26th July, is the location of the city's best pizza restaurant, Maison Thomas *(see p78)*; the only real Continental-style café, Simonds *(see p78)*; the best bookshop, Diwan *(see p75)*; and, in the back streets, countless small fashion boutiques and galleries.

View of a street in Zamalek

6 Manial Palace

The other island in the centre of the Nile, a little way south of Gezira, is Rhoda, worth visiting for the Manial Palace, which has been wonderfully restored. Built by Prince Mohammed Ali, uncle of King Farouk, between 1899 and 1929, it is a monument to excess and eccentric taste. Five pavilions are decorated in a variety of Islamic styles, including Moorish, Ottoman Turkish, Persian and Syrian. There is also a grotesque hunting museum that features hundreds of mounted ibex heads, as well as a hermaphrodite goat. *Map E6*

• Sharia al-Saray, Rhoda • 02 2368 7495 • Open 9am–4:30pm daily • Adm

Garden City

South of Midan Tahrir, Garden City is one of the most tranquil parts of central Cairo. It was created in the early 20th century by the British as a garden suburb with curving, tree-lined streets meant to evoke the country lanes of England. It is home to several embassies, including the British, Canadian and American.

7 Bulaq

Once the port of the Mamluk sultans, these days Bulaq is best known for the pandemonium of its *souqs*, which sell second-hand clothes and endless reams of cloth, as well as hardware, car parts and food. Not for the faint-hearted, this is another face of Cairo, bustling and un-touristy, yet hidden among the narrow alleys is the serenely perfect Mosque of Sinan Pasha. *Map F2*

8 Mahmoud Khalil Museum

Mohammed Mahmoud Khalil (1876–1953) was a politician and patron of the arts. He bequeathed his grand riverside home and the superb collection of sculpture and mostly French Impressionist and Post-Impressionist paintings it contained to the state. Here hang works by Corot, Ingres, Millet, Monet, Pissaro, Toulouse-Lautrec and Sisley. *Map D5*

• 1 Sharia Kafour, off Sharia al-Giza, Dokki • 02 3748 2142 • Currently closed due to theft • Adm

Mahmoud Khalil Museum

Pedestrian promenade by the Nile

9 The Nile

The Nile is the heart of Cairo, bisecting the city. On the east bank, the riverside Corniche al-Nil is one of the city's main north–south roads, making a walk beside the river anything but peaceful. However, over on Gezira, a pedestrian promenade runs along the water's edge. The best way to experience the river is to take a ride in a felucca, one of the small triangular-sailed boats used on the Nile since antiquity. They can be hired by the hour at landing stages in front of the Semiramis and Four Seasons Nile Plaza hotels *(see p125)*.

10 The Pyramids

Half a century ago the Pyramids were a daytrip out of Cairo. Now the city stretches out to the paws of the Sphinx. In a taxi on empty roads, from central Cairo to the Pyramids on Giza Plateau, takes 15 minutes. The roads are rarely empty, however, and the journey more often takes about an hour. It is worth the time in the car as there is more to see than just the Pyramids, including subsidiary temples, the Solar Boat Museum and the Sphinx *(see pp12–13)*.

A Morning Walk in "Paris on the Nile"

Beginning your walk at Midan Tahrir, walk north up Sharia Talaat Harb and stop at **Felfela Takeaway** (No. 15) *(see p78)* for a breakfast of *fuul* sandwiches. Ahead is **Midan Talaat Harb**, named for the nationalist banker whose statue stands in the middle of the square. Here on the left-hand side, golden Art Nouveau mosaics glitter around the entrance of Groppi, a patisserie and chocolatier in business on this site since 1925. Continue up Sharia Talaat Harb, passing on the right **El Abd bakery** (No. 25) *(see p77)*, makers of the best baklava and other Egyptian pastries in town. Cross the busy junction with Sharia Abd Al-Khaliq Sarwat and on the left, No. 34 is the **Yacoubian Building**, immortalized in the book and film of the same name *(see p49)*. The name is above the doorway in the entrance hall. Across the road is the Art Deco Cinema Metro, which opened in 1939 screening *Gone With the Wind*. Leave Sharia Talaat Harb and head east along Sharia Adly to pass the Babylonian-styled Shaar Hashamaim Synagogue, evidence of Egypt's one-time large and influential Jewish community. Bearing right at the next junction leads down to pretty Midan Mustafa Kamel; turn right again into Sharia Qasr al-Nil. Soon you reemerge at Midan Talaat Harb, at which point head south down Sharia Talaat Harb for lunch at **Café Riche** (No. 17) *(see p75)*, where the 1952 Revolution was supposedly plotted, and which has a wonderfully nostalgic vibe.

Left **Abdeen Palace Museum** Right **Islamic Ceramics Museum**

TOP 10 More Cairo Museums

1 Post Office Museum
Stamps and Egypt's oldest postboxes are displayed here. *Map H3 • Midan Ataba • 02 2391 0011 • Open 10am–2pm Sat–Thu • Adm*

2 Umm Kulsum Museum
A museum dedicated to the diva *(see p64)* exhibits her dresses, letters, press clippings and has a recordings archive. *Map L6 • Sharia al-Malik Salih, Rhoda • 02 2363 1537 • Open 9am–4pm • Adm*

3 Mahmoud Mokhtar Museum
Many works by Egypt's most famous sculptor *(see p64)* are shown in this museum, which doubles as the artist's mausoleum. *Map D4 • Sharia at-Tahrir, Gezira • 02 2735 2519 • Open 10am–6pm Tue–Thu, Sat & Sun • Adm*

4 Railway Museum
Adjacent to the Ramses train station is a hall with model trains, signalling devices and the private royal carriages of some of Egypt's former rulers. *Map G1 • Midan Ramses • Open 8am–2pm Tue–Sun • Adm*

5 Museum of Islamic Art
This is a superb museum of Islamic decorative arts *(see p46)*. *Map H4 • Midan Bab al-Khalq • 02 2390 9930 • Open 9am–4pm Sat–Thu, 9–11am, 2–4pm Fri • Adm*

6 Abdeen Palace Museum
A former royal palace, this museum houses silverware and chinaware. *Map G4 • Sharia Abd al-Raziq, Abdeen • 02 2391 0130 • Open 9am–3pm Sat–Thu • Adm*

7 Islamic Ceramics Museum
A 1920s villa used by Nasser as an office now houses historic ceramics from Egypt, Iran, Morocco and Andalucia. *Map D2 • Sharia al-Gezira, Zamalek • 02 2737 3298 • Currently closed due to theft • Adm*

8 Textiles Museum
Rare textiles from Pharaonic to Ottoman times are on show. *Map J3 • Sharia al-Muizz il-Din Allah • 02 2786 5227 • Open 9am–4:30pm daily • Adm*

9 Ethnological Museum
This museum is dedicated to Egyptian daily life, with a diorama of the opening of the Suez Canal. *Map F5 • 109 Al-Qasr al-Ainy • Open 9am–2:30pm Sat–Wed • Adm*

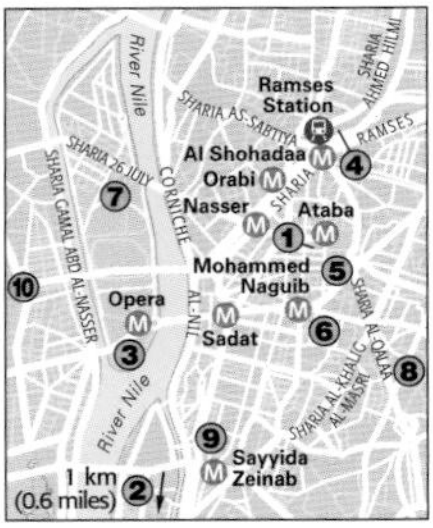

10 Agricultural Museum
Several museums on this site cover Bedouin traditions, the High Dam, mummified animals and much else. *Map H1 • Sharia Nadi al-Seid, Doqqi • 02 3337 2933 • Open 9am–2pm Tue–Thu & Sun • Adm*

For information on the main Cairo museums **see p46**

Left **Cairo Opera House** Right **Al-Sawy Culture Wheel**

TOP 10 Art and Culture Venues

1 Mashrabia Gallery
This gallery hosts temporary exhibitions of local and foreign artists. *Map F3 • 8 Sharia Champollion • 02 2578 4494 • Open 11am–8pm Sat–Thu • www.mashrabiagallery.org*

2 Townhouse Gallery
Cairo's most adventurous independent gallery shows the works of some of the city's best artists. *Map F3 • 10 Sharia Nabrawy, off Sharia Bassiouni • 02 2576 8086 • Open 10am–2pm, 6–9pm Sat–Wed, 6–9pm Fri • www.thetownhousegallery.com*

3 Al-Sawy Culture Wheel
The best venue in Cairo to catch live music has local bands and artists performing at least a couple of nights a week. *Map D2 • 1 Sharia 26th July, Zamalek • 02 2736 6178 • www.culturewheel.com/eng*

4 Makan
A small venue famous for its Tuesday and Wednesday folk music nights. *Map F5 • 1 Sharia Saad Zaghloul, Mounira • 02 2792 0878*

5 Cairo Jazz Club
Cairo's live jazz club has bands taking the stage four to six nights a week, performing mainly jazz, but also some blues and oriental music. *Map H1 • 197 Sharia 26th July, Agouza • 02 3345 9939 • Open 5pm–3am • www.cairojazzclub.com*

6 Diwan Bookshop
Cairo's best English-language bookshop sells DVDs and CDs too. *Map D2 • 159 Sharia 26th July, Zamalek • 02 2736 2598 • Open 9am–11:30pm*

7 Cairo Opera House
The city's main venue for opera, dance and classical music has several performance spaces, including an open-air amphitheatre *(see p71)*.

8 Museum of Modern Egyptian Art
The 400 pieces on display in this museum in the Cairo Opera House Grounds include work by the major figures of Egyptian art from the 20th century. Look out in particular for the work of Mahmoud Said (1897–1964) *(see p71)*.

9 Arabic Music Institute
The institute houses a sound archive of oriental music, a museum devoted to composer Abdel Wahab and a concert space. *Map F3 • Sharia Ramses, just north of Sharia 26th July • 02 2574 3373 • Open 10am–2:30pm Sat–Thu • www.cairoopera.org/arab_music.aspx • Adm*

10 Café Riche
Somewhat of a national monument, this historic café is a haunt of intellectuals, writers and artists. *Map F4 • 17 Sharia Talaat Harb • 02 2392 9793 • Open 10am–midnight*

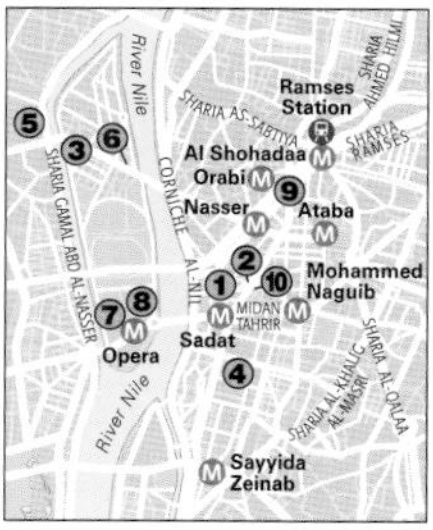

Left **Heba Linens** Right **Bedouin-style jewellery at Nomad**

TOP 10 Places to Shop

1 Nomad
Nomad specializes in Bedouin-style jewellery, traditional crafts, and clothes – a great shop for unique gifts. *Map E2 • Cairo Marriott, 16 Sharia Saraya al-Gezira, Zamalek (also at 14 Sharia Saraya al-Gezira, Zamalek)*

2 Azza Fahmy Boutique
This boutique sells the work of Egypt's best-known jeweller, Azza Fahmy, whose stylish pieces consist of traditional elements and motifs with a contemporary twist. *Map D1 • 15C Sharia Taha Hussein, cnr of Sharia Mohammed Marashli, Zamalek*

3 Heba Linens
This is the shop for excellent-quality Egyptian cotton goods, including sheets and towels. *Map E1 • Second Floor, Arcadia Mall, Corniche al-Nil, Boulaq (other branches in the City Stars Mall, the Semiramis Hotel and the Four Seasons First Residence)*

4 And Company
This store is full of quality cottons, beautiful artworks, ceramics and gifts. *Map D1 • 3A Sharia Baghat Ali, Zamalek*

5 Lehnert & Landrock
A large selection of prints of historic black and white images of Egypt can be found in this downtown bookshop. *Map G3 • 44 Sharia Sherif, Downtown*

6 Sound of Cairo (Sot al-Qahira)
This is probably the best shop for Arabic music, classical or pop, and has an extensive stock. Look for a white-painted frontage with red Arabic lettering. *Map F3 • 3 Sharia al-Borsa al-Gedida, off Sharia Qasr al-Nil, Downtown*

7 Bashayer
This shop sells all things oriental, including ceramics, carved wooden items, copper lamps, leather bags and rich fabrics. Doqqi is a 10-minute taxi ride from Midan Tahrir. *58 Sharia Mosaddeq, Doqqi*

8 Al Qahira
Beautifully crafted goods, from clothes to furnishings, incorporating traditional Arabic and modern Egyptian elements. *Map D1 • 6 Sharia Bahgat Ali, Zamalek*

9 Oum El Dounia
This is a treasure-trove of handicrafts from all over Egypt and Nubia, with a Francophone ambiance. *Map F4 • 1st Floor, 3 Sharia Talaat Harb, Downtown*

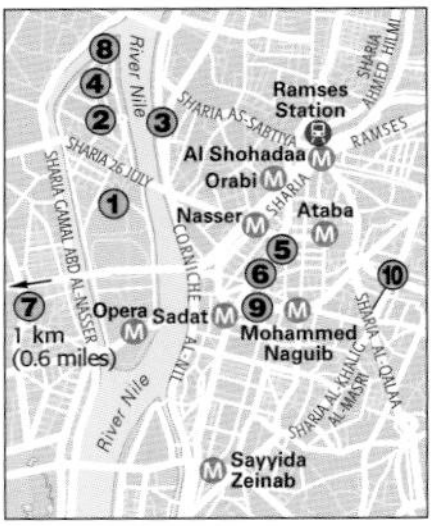

10 Sharia Al-Qalaa
This street has at least a dozen shops that sell traditional musical instruments, such as the *oud* (lute). Many of the street's cafés are musicians' haunts. *Map H3–5 • Sharia Al-Qalaa, off Midan Ataba, Downtown*

Left **Smoking sheesha** Centre **Pastries at El-Abd** Right **Feluccas on the Nile**

TOP 10 Unmissable Experiences

1 Drifting in a Felucca

After a hard day's sightseeing there's no better way to unwind than by drifting on the Nile in your own private boat. For information about where to hire a felucca see p73.

2 Hearing the Muezzins' Chorus at Dusk

You can't fail to hear the muezzins' haunting dusk chorus every evening, but to hear a particularly memorable rendition, be at the top of the Cairo Tower as the sun goes down *(see p71)*.

3 Friday Prayers Downtown

About the only time that the chaos of Downtown Cairo quietens is at noon every Friday for prayers. The traffic is brought to a standstill as devout Muslims roll their prayer mats out in the street and prostrate themselves.

4 Pastries from El-Abd

This bakery is probably the most popular shop in all of Cairo. Squeeze yourself in and order a quarter kilo of *baklava* or *konafa*. *Map F3 • 25 Sharia Talaat Harb, Downtown*

5 Late-night Pizza at Maison Thomas

Cairo truly does not sleep. People are out on the streets chatting and socializing until the early hours. Many food places are open way beyond midnight, if not 24 hours, including this pizzeria and deli in Zamalek *(see p78)*.

6 Smoking Sheesha

Once the preserve of adult males, now everyone smokes *sheesha*. You can do so at any coffee house, but you may prefer the more hygienic surroundings of a hotel coffee house or upmarket restaurant such as Abu al-Sid *(see p79)*. The most popular flavour for novices is *tufah* (apple).

7 Whirling Dervishes

On Monday, Wednesday and Saturday evenings, the Wikala al-Ghouri hosts the Al Tanoura Sufi dancers, some of whom can spin for over 30 minutes. Arrive by 6:30pm for a free ticket *(see p15)*.

8 Friday Afternoon Football at a Coffee House

For an electric atmosphere, take a seat at any busy coffee house, particularly those at the top end of Sharia Talaat Harb, on a Friday afternoon during the local football season (August–May). *Map F–G3 • Sharia Talaat Harb, Downtown*

9 A Beer in the Garden of the Cairo Marriott

The lovely garden terrace at this hotel is a great place for a beer after a day's sightseeing *(see p125)*.

10 A Night at a Belly-Dancing Club

Sheherazade on Sharia Alfy Bey is a notorious belly-dancing club which makes for a colourful and memorable night out. *Map G3 • 1 Sharia Alfy Bey, Downtown*

Left **Maison Thomas** Centre **Abou Tarek Koshari** Right **A coffee at Cilantro**

Top 10 Cafés and Streetfood

1 Felfela Takeaway

This is a favourite stop-off for *fuul* and *taamiya* sandwiches, as well as chicken and lamb *shawarma*. *Map F4 • 15 Sharia Talaat Harb, Downtown • £*

2 Abou Tarek Koshari

The king of *koshari* has been in business since 1950 and this is Cairo's biggest and smartest *koshari* outlet. A very filling meal costs only a couple of Egyptian pounds. *Map F3 • 16 Sharia Maarouf, cnr of Sharia Champollion, Downtown • 02 2577 5935 • £*

3 Cairo Kitchen

This youthful place has made *koshari* cool. Also on the menu is a range of salads. *Map D2 • 118 Sharia 26th July (entrance on Sharia Aziz Osman), Zamalek • 02 2735 4000 • ££*

4 Maison Thomas

Reputedly in business since 1929, this is still the best pizza restaurant in Cairo. Take away or eat on the premises in a European-style deli interior. Hot and cold sandwiches are also available. *Map E2 • 157 Sharia 26th July, Zamalek • 02 2735 7057 • Open 24 hours daily • £££*

5 Fatatri Pizza at-Tahrir

This restaurant serves both savoury and sweet *fiteer*. *Map F4 • Sharia at-Tahrir • Open 24 hours daily • £*

6 Cilantro

This is one of several branches of a smart coffee house chain, which also serves cakes and sandwiches and has Wi-Fi and local English-language newspapers and magazines. *Map D2 • 157 Sharia 26th July, Zamalek • 02 2736 1115 • ££*

7 Simonds

This is the closest to an authentic Italian espresso bar in Cairo. *Map D2 • 112 Sharia 26th July, Zamalek • 02 2735 9436 • £*

8 Mandarin Khadeer

Refreshing and delicious fruit sorbets and ice creams are the main attraction of this Zamalek institution, but there are plenty of sticky pastries on offer as well. *Map D1 • 17 Sharia Shagarat al-Dor, Zamalek • £*

9 Akher Saa

This popular *fuul* and *taamiya* takeaway also has a sit-down restaurant area. *Map G3 • 8 Sharia Alfy Bey, Downtown • Open 24 hours daily • £*

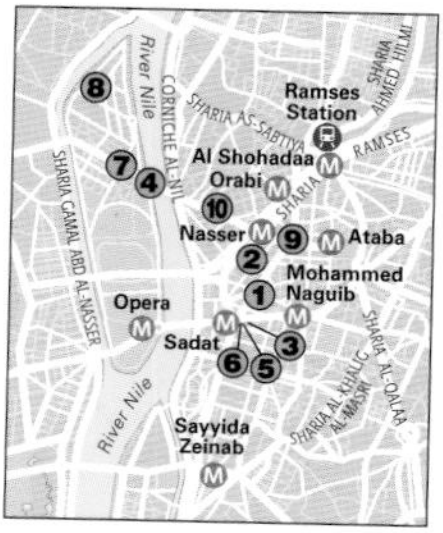

10 Gad

This is another takeaway with a sit-down restaurant attached, and it has a particularly extensive menu. *Map F3 • 13 Sharia 26th July, Downtown • 02 2576 3353 • Open 24 hours daily • ££*

For information on Egyptian dishes **see pp58–9**

Price Categories
For a two-course meal for one with a soft drink and including service.
£ under £E30
££ £E30–60
£££ £E60–120
££££ £E120–250
£££££ over £E250

Above **Osmanly at the Kempinski Nile Hotel**

Top 10 Restaurants

1 Abu al-Sid

One of Cairo's most fashionable restaurants has a menu of Egyptian classics. Alcohol is served, as is *sheesha (see p60)*. *Map D2 • 157 Sharia 26th July, Zamalek • 02 2735 9640 • ££££*

2 Aqua at the Four Seasons Nile Plaza

Dine at one of Cairo's top hotels *(see p125)*, where the seafood menu includes lobster. Excellent steaks are also served *(see p60)*. *Map E5 • Four Seasons at the Nile Plaza, 1089 Corniche al-Nil, Garden City • 02 2791 6900 • Closed lunch • £££££*

3 Buddha Bar

With an exceptional Nile-side setting, sublime Asian food and great music, this is the coolest place in Cairo *(see p60)*. *Map E5 • Sofitel el-Gezira, 3 Sharia el-Thawra Council, Gezira • 02 2737 3737 • ££££*

4 Felfela

Felfela is treasured for its bric-a-brac decor and menu of Egyptian staples *(see p60)*. *Map F4 • 15 Sharia Hoda Sharaawi, Downtown • 02 2392 2751 • ££*

5 La Bodega

This smart restaurant serves international dishes hard to find elsewhere in Cairo *(see p61)*. *Map E2 • Baehler's Mansions, 157 Sharia 26th July, Zamalek • 02 2735 0543 • ££££*

6 Osmanly at the Kempinski Nile Hotel

This restaurant, in a top hotel *(see p125)*, serves food inspired by the Ottoman sultans. It is open from 4pm. *Map E1 • Corniche al-Nil, 12 Sharia Ahmed Ragheb, Garden City • 02 2798 0000 • £££££*

7 L'Aubergine

One of the few restaurants in Egypt to cater for vegetarians is this small eatery with an upstairs bar and a downstairs dining area. The menu changes regularly. *Map D2 • 5 Sharia Sayed al-Bakri, Zamalek • 02 2738 0080 • £££*

8 Taboula

Serving the best Lebanese food in the city, this charming basement restaurant is warmly inviting. Alcohol is served. *Map E5 • 1 Sharia Latin American, Garden City • 02 2624 5722 • £££*

9 Abu Shakra

This popular chain serves charcoal-grilled meat for takeaway or a sit-down meal. *Map F5 • 69 Sharia Qasr al-Ainy, Downtown • 02 2531 6111 • £££*

10 Andrea

This open-air garden restaurant near the Pyramids serves grilled chicken and freshly baked bread. *Map H2 • 59–60 Marioutiya Canal, Giza • 02 3383 1133 • £££*

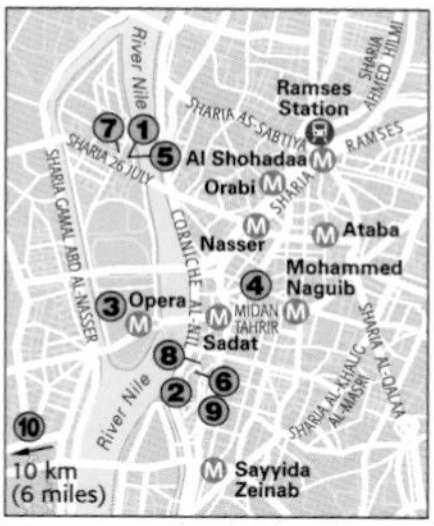

Left **Mosque of Amr** Right **Al-Azhar Park**

The Old City

A ROMAN FORTRESS ORIGINALLY STOOD ON THE SITE OF CAIRO. *Known as Babylon-in-Egypt, it guarded a Nile crossing on the route to the ancient Egyptian capital of Memphis* (see p91). *This was surrendered to the invading armies of Islam in AD 640, who set up camp next door. The camp was made permanent and was expanded north by successive Arab dynasties, culminating in the walled city of Al-Qahira in 969. It is this area, from Babylon in the south, now known as Coptic Cairo or Old Cairo, to the northern gates of Al-Qahira, now known as Islamic Cairo, that make up the venerable core of today's city, representing almost 1,400 years of continuously inhabited history – a mere fraction of the age of the Pyramids, but certainly worth a few days of exploration.*

A view of Islamic Cairo

Carved stonework, Northern Cemetery

TOP 10 Sights

1. Islamic Cairo
2. Khan al-Khalili
3. The Citadel
4. Al-Azhar Park
5. Coptic Cairo
6. Coptic Museum
7. Mosque of Amr
8. Mosque of Ibn Tulun
9. Mosque of Sultan Hassan
10. Northern Cemetery

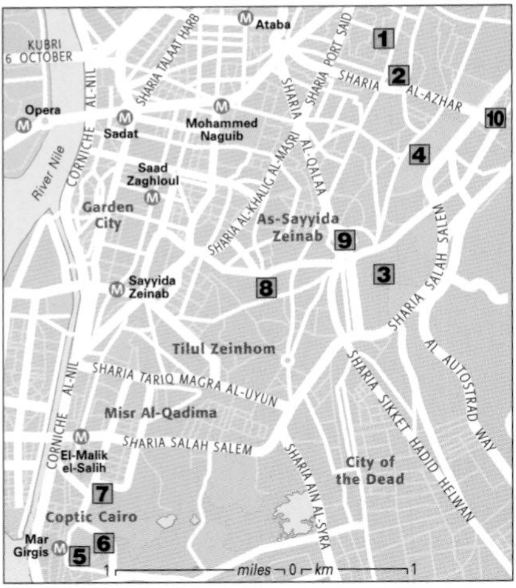

Preceding pages **View from the courtyard of Al-Azhar Mosque, Cairo**

1 Islamic Cairo

Stretching several miles along a north–south axis in the east of Cairo, this part of the city retains its medieval street pattern. The main streets are being restored, but most neighbourhoods remain ramshackle, housing a way of life largely unchanged in centuries. Streets are studded with several hundred monuments, from Ottoman-era fountains to splendid Mamluk palace complexes, most of which are accessible to visitors *(see p87)*. At the heart of it all is Khan al-Khalili souq and Al-Azhar Mosque *(see pp14–15)*.

2 Khan al-Khalili

This is Cairo's chaotic and vibrant bazaar area, parts of which date back to the 16th century. Its covered passageways, stone gates and labyrinthine alleys still have a wholly medieval feel. The trade in spices, brightly coloured cloth, perfumes, gold and silver bears little relation to the Western department store or supermarket. Of course, you have to haggle – you will pay over the odds if you don't – but it's all part of the theatre. *Map J3 • Some shops closed Sun am*

Khan al-Khalili

Mosque of Suleyman Pasha in the Citadel

3 The Citadel

Overlooking the city from a rocky spur of the Muqattam Hills, the Citadel is a sizeable fortress. Founded in the 12th century, it served as the royal residence and barracks until the late 1800s. Its earliest parts date back to the reign of the ruler Salah ad-Din (Saladin), but over the course of its history it was reorganized and enlarged on numerous occasions. There are three mosques to visit, as well as former palace buildings and museums *(see p86)*. *Map J6 • Sharia Salah Salem • Open 8am–5pm • Adm*

4 Al-Azhar Park

This beautiful park features a tall grassy hill at one end that slopes down to an artificial lake at the other end. It is landscaped in classical Islamic fashion with water features and flower beds, but also has an amphitheatre, children's play area, a fine restaurant *(see p89)* and cafés. The views over Islamic Cairo are superb *(see p56)*.

The Copts

Before the arrival of Islam, Egypt was Christian and its people were known as Copts. When the Arab army occupied Egypt in AD 640, its leader Amr instructed his people to take good care of the Copts, for the Prophet himself had given orders for them to do so. Today Copts make up 10 per cent of the nation.

5 Coptic Cairo

The heart of the district of Cairo's Coptic Christian community centres on the Roman fortress of Babylon. The ancient gate towers of the former fortress provide access to a sunken compound (evidence that the street level has risen over the centuries), containing the Coptic Museum, numerous churches, a synagogue and several cemeteries *(see p88)*.
Map M6 • www.coptic-cairo.com

6 Coptic Museum

Founded in 1908, the museum houses an absorbing collection representing a key period in world history, when the old gods were being replaced by Christianity. It is housed in a beautiful building, with exquisite painted ceilings and *mashrabiya* windows. The Old Wing gives access to a Roman tower known as the Water Gate.
Map M6 • Sharia Mar Girgis • 02 2362 9742 • Open 9am–4pm (5pm in summer) • www.coptic-cairo.com • Adm

7 Mosque of Amr

Egypt's oldest mosque was founded by Amr Ibn al-As, the Arab general who conquered Egypt for Islam in AD 640. Although it has been altered many times since and doubled in size in 827, the Mosque of Amr today represents the beginnings of Islam in Egypt. It remains a very simple and humble structure. Behind the mosque, which is just a few minutes' walk north of Coptic Cairo, the surrounding hard-mud wasteland is the site of Fustat, the first Arab city in Egypt. *Map M5 • Sharia Mar Girgis • Closed for midday prayers Fri*

8 Mosque of Ibn Tulun

Successive Arab dynasties expanded the original city of Fustat north. One of these was the Tulunid dynasty (AD 868–905), founded by Ibn Tulun, who was sent to Egypt to govern on behalf of the Abbasids of Baghdad. His splendid mosque echoes those of his homeland of Iraq in its unique (for Egypt) minaret, which has a staircase spiralling around the outside of the tower. It is possible to climb the minaret to admire the view, not least of the mosque's great courtyard with its elegant arcades and fine central ablutions fountain. Next to the mosque is the Gayer-Anderson Museum *(see p46)*. *Map G6 • Sharia Abdel Meguid • Open 8am–5pm daily*

View from inside the courtyard of the Mosque of Ibn Tulun

Interior of the Mosque of Sultan Hassan

9 Mosque of Sultan Hassan

After Al-Azhar *(see pp14–15)*, the other essential mosque to visit is that of Sultan Hassan. Begun in 1356, its size rivals the great cathedrals of Europe. It is entered through a soaring portal with a stalactite hood, which leads to a simple but impressive courtyard with four massive arched recesses. The sultan lies at rest in his tomb chamber, to the right of the prayer niche. The neighbouring mosque, Al-Rifai, although similar in scale to Sultan Hassan, was built over 500 years later. *Map H5 • Midan Salah ad-Din • Open 8am–4:30pm (closed for midday prayers Fri) • Adm*

10 Northern Cemetery

A lack of space caused Cairo's medieval rulers to build their funerary monuments outside the city walls in the desert. Here they created some of Cairo's finest medieval monuments, from modest single-chambered tombs to palatial complexes with multiple courts, minarets and domes. Less exalted personages chose to be buried here also, beside their rulers. Over the centuries the homeless have moved into the tombs to the point today where the cemetery is a vibrant and living neighbourhood, usually referred to as the City of the Dead. *Map Q3–6*

A Stroll up the Main Street of Medieval Cairo

Take a taxi to "Al-Hussein". You will be let out beside the **Mosque of Al-Azhar** *(see pp14–15)*; walk to a footbridge over the road, cross and take the side street immediately in front, from where you emerge onto Sharia al-Muiz li-Din Allah, the main street of medieval Cairo. You can buy spices, silver, gold, brass or copper ware at the many stalls in **Khan al-Khalili** *(see p15)*. Continue up the street, to find, one next to the other, the **Madrassa–Mausoleum of Sultan Qalaoun**, the **Mosque of an-Nasir Mohammed** and the **Madrassa of Sultan Barquq**. These are three splendid monuments from the Mamluk era, all of which can be visited *(see p87)*.

A short distance ahead, the road divides at a small building with big grilled windows on the right-hand side: this is the **Sabil-Kuttab of Abdel Rahman Katkhuda** *(see p87)*. Bear left and continue, passing the small **Mosque of Al-Aqmar** *(see p87)*, then take Darb al-Asfur on the right to visit a fine old merchant's house, **Beit al-Suhaymi** *(see p87)*, where you can have tea in the courtyard.

Return to Sharia al-Muiz li-Din Allah. After a short time the road widens into a piazza beside the walls of the **Mosque of Al-Hakim** *(see p87)*, built by a Fatimid sultan. The mosque abuts the **Northern Walls** *(see p87)* of the original city of Al-Qahira; you can access the ramparts via the nearby gates *(see p87)*. Return the way you came, treating yourself to lunch at the **Naguib Mahfouz Café** in Khan al-Khalili *(see p89)*.

Left **The Citadel walls** Right **Mosque of Mohammed Ali**

TOP 10 The Citadel

1 Mosque of Mohammed Ali
Built between 1824 and 1848, this grand Turkish-style mosque continues to dominate the Cairo skyline. Mohammed Ali is buried in a white marble cenotaph just inside the entrance.

2 Mosque of Sultan al-Nasir
This low-rise building behind the Mohammed Ali Mosque is more than 500 years older than its neighbour, dating back to 1318–35. Its ribbed minarets have beautiful Persian tiling.

3 Gawhara Palace
South of the Mohammed Ali Mosque, this small palace is decorated in a French style and its rooms contain displays of 19th-century furniture and dress.

4 Prison Museum
Until 1952 the Citadel was a British army barracks. You can peep into the cells where prisoners were once detained. The most famous detainee was Anwar Sadat, who later became president of Egypt (1970–1981) but who was arrested for revolutionary activities.

5 Police Museum
This single-room museum covers some of Egypt's most sensational crimes, including those of Raya and Sakina, Alexandrian sisters who were serial killers and who murdered 30 women before being captured and executed in 1921.

6 Military Museum
The Citadel's main building houses a collection of ceremonial uniforms and arms, as well as a large-scale model of the fortress.

7 Mosque of Suleyman Pasha
This small 16th-century mosque was built in a Turkish style soon after the Ottoman takeover of Egypt. The underside of its dome is beautifully decorated.

8 The Walls
The walls were begun by Salah Al-Din and expanded by his nephew A-Kamil. It is possible to vist the interiors of some towers.

9 Carriage Museum
This building (currently closed) decorated with a row of horse-heads houses six royal carriages, the largest of which was given to the Khedive Ismail by Napoleon IIII.

10 The Terraces
The views from the terraces by the Mohammed Ali Mosque across Cairo to the Pyramids are spectacular on a clear day.

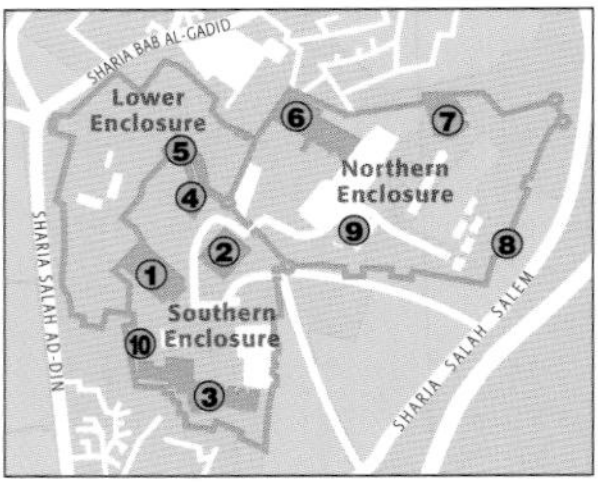

For general background information about the Citadel **see p83**

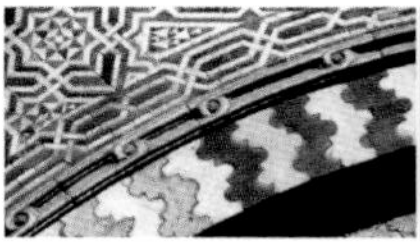

Left **Mausoleum of Qalaoun** Centre **Mosque of Al-Aqmar** Right **Sabil-Kuttab of Abdel Katkhuda**

TOP 10 More Islamic Monuments

1 Madrassa–Mausoleum of Sultan Qalaoun
Built in just 13 months in 1284–5, this grand complex marries scale with fantastic detailing, particularly in the sultan's mausoleum. *Map J3 • Sharia al-Muizz li-Din Allah*

2 Mosque of al-Nasir Mohammed
This mosque, built during the reign of Al-Nasir Mohammed (1293–1340), a son of Qalaoun, is noteworthy for its minaret, which has fabulously intricate, lace-like decoration in a Moorish style. *Map J3 • Sharia al-Muizz li-Din Allah*

3 Madrassa of Sultan Barquq
This grand religious school was completed in 1386. It is possible to go up to the roof and ascend the minaret. *Map J3 • Sharia al-Muizz li-Din Allah*

4 Sabil-Kuttab of Abdel Rahman Katkhuda
This graceful Ottoman structure was a charitable institution funded by a nobleman. The *sabil* (public fountain) was on the ground floor, while the *kuttab* (primary school) was upstairs. *Map J3 • Sharia al-Muizz li-Din Allah*

5 Mosque of Al-Aqmar
This pretty mosque supposedly gets its name ("the moonlit") from the way its masonry would shine in the moonlight. It is one of the oldest buildings in the area, dating back to 1125. *Map J3 • Sharia al-Muizz li-Din Allah*

6 Beit al-Suhaymi
Visit this restored house to see how a wealthy merchant lived in the 18th century. It is also the venue for free weekly concerts of Arabic music, every Sunday at 8pm. *Map J3 • 19 Darb al-Asfur, off Sharia al-Muizz li-Din Allah • Open 9am–5pm • Adm*

7 Mosque of Al-Hakim
The Fatimid caliph Al-Hakim bi-Amr Allah (996–1021) was infamous for his strange laws and random acts of violence. His mosque is noted for its odd pepper-pot minarets. *Map J3 • Sharia al-Muizz li-Din Allah*

8 Northern Walls
The northern walls date from 1087 and are the most complete part of the fortifications that once encircled Al-Qahira. They include two gates via which you can ascend to the ramparts. *Map J3 • Sharia al-Galai • Adm*

9 Mosque, Madrassa and Mausoleum of Al-Ghouri
The striped twin buildings of this stunning complex were built in 1505 by the last Mamluk sultan Al-Ghouri. *Map J4 • Sharia al-Muizz li-Din Allah • Open 9am–5pm • Adm*

10 Bab Zuweyla
This is one of the original gates of the city of Qahira. Its two minarets were added later – they can be ascended for marvellous views over Islamic Cairo. *Map J4 • Sharia Ahmed Mahir • Adm*

For more information on Islamic Cairo **see pp82–5**

Left **An Orthodox cemetery** Centre **Church of St Barbara** Right **Hanging Church**

Top 10 Coptic Cairo

1 Hanging Church
Suspended above the compound's Water Gate *(see p84)*, parts of this church may date back to the 4th century. Look out for the black thirteenth pillar supporting the pulpit, representing Judas. *Map M6 • Open 9am–5pm. Coptic mass: 8am Fri, 7am Sun*

2 Roman Towers
The main entrance to the Coptic Cairo compound is between the two circular towers of Babylon's western gate. The righthand tower is in ruins, while the other forms the base of the Church of St George. *Map M6*

3 Church of St George
This is the only round church in Egypt, built that way because it sits on one of the original fortress gate towers. The current church dates to 1904, replacing a 10th-century church destroyed by fire. *Map M6 • Open 8:30am–4pm*

4 Convent of St George
Although still a working nunnery, several rooms are open to visitors, including a medieval hall and a chapel with a casket claimed to contain relics of St George. *Map M6 • Open 9am–4pm*

5 Church of St Sergius
Sunk below street level, this 5th-century church is Egypt's oldest. Steps descend to a crypt where the Holy Family is supposed to have taken shelter. *Map M6 • Open 8am–4pm*

6 Church of the Virgin
This small 18th-century church is notable for several fine icons. *Map M6 • Open 9am–4pm*

7 Church of St Barbara
This lovely 11th-century church, dedicated to a 3rd-century saint who was executed for preaching Christianity, houses some fine icons, although the most precious items were removed to the Coptic Museum *(see p84)*. *Map M6 • Open 8am–8pm*

8 Ben Ezra Synagogue
Originally a church sold to pay off taxes, this building became a synagogue in AD 882. In the 1990s it was extensively and lavishly restored. *Map M6 • Open 9am–4pm*

9 The Cemeteries
East of the Coptic Museum and churches are three conjoined cemeteries still used by people of the Greek Orthodox, Greek Catholic and Coptic faiths. Many of the tombs are marked with statues and mausolea. *Map M5–6*

10 Nilometer
Near Coptic Cairo, cut into the bedrock at the southern tip of Rhoda, this was used to record the rising of the Nile water by the ancient Egyptians. Its present form dates to the 9th century and is decorated with Koranic verses. *Map L6 • Sharia al-Malik Salih, Rhoda • Open 9am–5pm • Adm*

For general background information on Coptic Cairo **see pp84–5**

Above **Fishawi's**

Price Categories

For a two-course meal for one with a soft drink and including service.

£	under £E30
££	£E30–60
£££	£E60–120
££££	£E120–250
£££££	over £E250

Top 10 Cafés and Restaurants

1 Fishawi's
Cairo's oldest and most famed coffee house fills a narrow alley in Khan al-Khalili. It claims never to have closed in over 200 years. *Map J4 • Midan al-Hussein • £*

2 Egyptian Pancake House
This popular eatery serves *fiteer* topped with your choice of cheese, egg, tomato and ground meat. For dessert, choose from raisins, coconut and icing sugar. *Map J4 • Midan al-Hussein • ££*

3 Naguib Mahfouz Café
Providing air-conditioned tranquility in the middle of Khan al-Khalili, this café with copper-top tables serves mainly sandwiches and refreshing cold drinks. *Map J3 • 5 Siqqet al-Badestan • 02 2590 3788 • ££*

4 Khan al-Khalili Restaurant
Adjacent to and under the same management as the Naguib Mahfouz Café, this restaurant serves international and Egyptian dishes, notably grilled meats. *Map J3 • 5 Siqqet al-Badestan • 02 2590 3788 • ££££*

5 Citadel View Studio Misr
In a grand faux-Mamluk building, and with commanding views over Islamic Cairo and the Al-Azhar Park, this restaurant serves grilled meats and meze. It has a terrace for alfresco eating too. *Map J4 • Al-Azhar Park, Sharia Salah Salem • ££££*

6 Al-Dahan
Serving some of the best basic *kofta* and kebabs in Midan al-Hussein, Al-Dahan can be found underneath the Al-Hussein Hotel. *Map J4 • Midan al-Hussein, entered from the passage that leads to Fishawi's coffee house • ££*

7 Lakeside Café
This pleasant café occupying several pavilions and a courtyard overlooking a man-made lake in Al-Azhar Park serves light Oriental meals and snacks. *Map J4 • Al-Azhar Park, Sharia Salah Salem • 02 2510 9162 • £££*

8 Gad
A branch of the popular *fuul* and *taamiya* chain that has restaurants all over Cairo *(see p78)*. *Map J4 • Sharia al-Azhar, near Al-Azhar mosque • ££*

9 Abu Bassem Grill
This restaurant serves great kebabs and meze and has an outside area, while diners inside can enjoy the restaurant's medieval interior. *Map J4 • 2 Zuqqaq al-Gahini, Midan al-Hussein • ££*

10 Rifai
This humble eatery at which diners sit at tables laid out in the street is regarded by many Cairenes as the city's best kebab restaurant. *Map G5 • Sharia al-Barrani (opposite the Sayyida Zeinab mosque), Midan Sayyida Zeinab • Closed lunch • ££*

For information about Egyptian dishes see **pp58–9**

Left **View across the Suez Canal from Port Said** Right **Red Pyramid, Dahsur**

Beyond Cairo

CAIRO LIES JUST SOUTH OF THE POINT AT WHICH THE NILE DIVIDES *into two main branches that create a fertile fan between them, known as the Delta, spreading north to the Mediterranean. This is an area in which life has flourished throughout history. The apex of the Delta was the site of the first great imperial city of ancient Egypt, Memphis, which has now almost completely vanished. We get some intimation of its glory and vastness thanks to the city's great necropolises of Saqqara and the various pyramid fields that remain. The Delta itself was where later pharaohs created new capitals, Alexander founded his new city, Alexandria (at the point at which the Delta met the sea) and early Christianity flourished. All of these places can be visited as day trips from Cairo.*

Colonial architecture, Ismailia

TOP 10 Sights

1. **Memphis**
2. **Saqqara**
3. **Dahshur**
4. **Fayoum**
5. **Port Said**
6. **Ismailia**
7. **Wadi Natrun**
8. **Abu Sir**
9. **Birqash Camel Market**
10. **Alexandria**

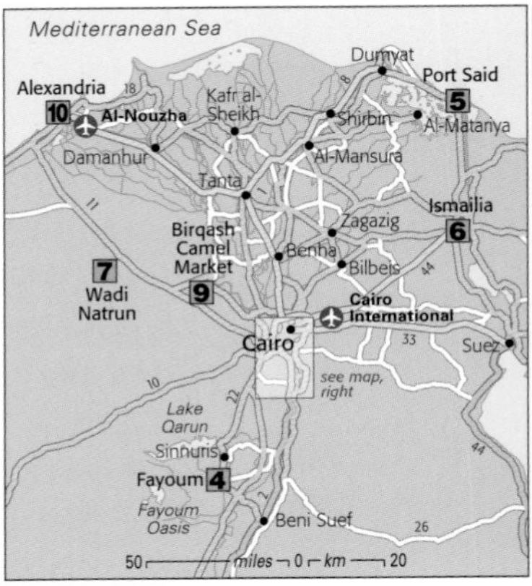

1 Memphis

Not much remains of the ancient city of Memphis, the capital of Egypt during the Old Kingdom. It is thought to have been founded about 3100 BC by King Menes, the ruler who united Upper And Lower Egypt. From historical accounts we know that it was a city of grand palaces and temples, which were all torn down by foreign invaders from the Romans onwards, and the ruins were buried. What remains today is gathered in a small open-air museum, the centrepiece of which is a colossal statue of Ramses II, which lies in its own special viewing pavilion. *Map J2 • Off Hwy 27, 47 km (29 miles) S of Cairo • Open 8am–4pm • Adm*

2 Saqqara

One of the richest archaeological sites in Egypt, Saqqara was the royal burial ground for some of the earliest rulers and their courtiers. This is the site of Egypt's prototype pyramid, a stepped structure built for King Djoser. The necropolis remained in use for some 3,000 years throughout the Pharaonic era, with additions being made as late as the Graeco-Roman period. It merits at least half a day's visit *(see p94)*. *Map J2 • Off Hwy 27, 44 km (27 miles) S of Cairo • Open 8am–5pm in summer (until 4pm in winter) • Adm*

Step Pyramid of Djoser, Saqqara

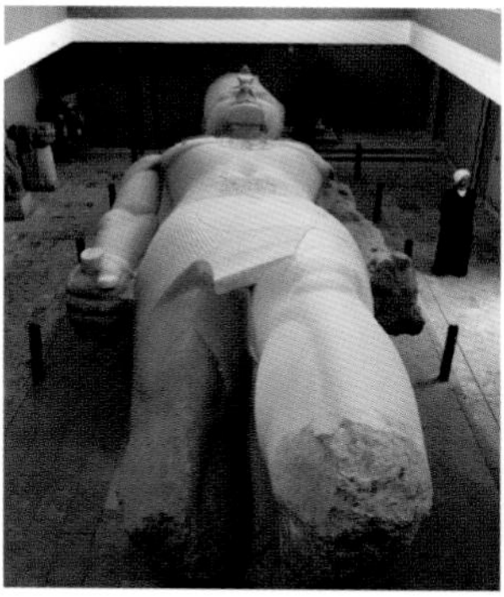

Colossus of Ramses II, Memphis

3 Dahshur

The two pyramids at Dahshur were built by the 4th-Dynasty king Sneferu, father of Khufu, the builder of the Great Pyramid *(see pp12–13)*. The Bent Pyramid, thus known because its sides start steeply, then switch part way to a shallower slope, is considered to be Egypt's first proper pyramid, as before this all pyramids were stepped. The other monument, known as the Red Pyramid due to its ancient red graffiti, can be entered and explored. *Map H2 • Off Hwy 27, 64 km (40 miles) S of Cairo • Open 9am–5pm in summer (until 4pm in winter) • Adm*

4 Fayoum

Fayoum is Egypt's largest oasis and a popular spot for second homes for Cairenes. A prime location is a site overlooking Lake Qarun, which is at the heart of the oasis and home to an amazing variety of bird species. Visitors should head for Kom Aushim, where you can visit the remains of 3rd-century BC crocodile temples – the Greeks named this area Crocodilopolis, after the animals that lived in the lake (now long gone). *Map A2 • Off Hwy 27, 100 km (62 miles) S of Cairo*

Deir Anba Bishoi monastery, Wadi Natrun

5 Port Said

Founded in 1859 to house Suez Canal workers, Port Said is a major harbour. Its most prominent building is the green-domed Suez Canal Authority Building, from where all shipping is monitored. The fish restaurants are Egypt's best and the Military Museum is worth a visit *(see p93)*. *Map B1 • 225 km (139 miles) NE of Cairo*

6 Ismailia

Halfway along the Suez Canal, Ismailia was founded to house the workers on the canal in the 1860s. It is a pretty town, with plenty of greenery surrounding European-style houses. The Ismailia Museum houses Graeco-Roman artefacts and items relating to the canal's history. *Map B1 • 120 km (74 miles) NE of Cairo • Ismailia Museum, Sharia Salah Salem, Open 9am–4pm Sat–Thu, 9–11am & 1–4pm Fri, Adm*

Egypt and the Camel

Although it has become part of the iconography of Egypt, the camel is not native to the country. In fact, it is a relative latecomer. Pharaonic tomb paintings show lions and hippos, as well as other creatures now extinct in Egypt, but not camels, which were then unknown. Historians believe that they were introduced by the invading Persians.

7 Wadi Natrun

Prized by the ancient Egyptians as a source of the salt deposit natron, a vital ingredient in the mummification process, this remote valley just west of the Delta region was later equally valued by the early Christians as a hiding place from persecution by the Romans. Initially they sheltered in caves, later building monasteries, of which four remain today. Each monastery has a full complement of monks and three of the monasteries welcome visitors. *Map A2 • Off Desert Hwy, 100 km (62 miles) NW of Cairo*

8 Abu Sir

The four pyramids at Abu Sir were built in the 5th Dynasty, and therefore date after the three great monuments at Giza. These pyramids are much smaller than their Giza counterparts and are very dilapidated. However, the isolated location on a sandy desert ridge rising away from the palm groves of the Nile plain lends this little visited site great charm. The northernmost and best-preserved Pyramid of Sahure can be entered, although this is not recommended for claustrophobics. *Map J2 • Off Hwy 27, 27 km (17 miles) S of Cairo • Open 8am–sunset • Adm*

9 Birqash Camel Market

A visit to Egypt's largest camel market is a truly memorable experience. Hundreds of camels are sold at Birqash every Monday and Friday morning (the main day is Friday). The camels are brought in their thousands from northwestern Sudan in a month-long trek to Aswan, from where they are then trucked up to Cairo. They are bought as mounts, but also for their meat. The best way to get to the market is by organized tour or a taxi hired for half a day. *Map A2 • Off Mansuriya Canal Road, 30 km (18 miles) NW of Cairo • Open mornings from 6am Mon & Fri • Adm*

Birqash Camel Market

10 Alexandria

After defeating the Persians in 332 BC, Alexander the Great founded his new capital city on the Mediterranean coast that same year. Under his successor Ptolemy and the dynasty he founded, it became the most important city of the ancient world – an economic, political and cultural rival to Rome. After falling into decline in the 4th century, it was revived in the 19th century, drawing thousands of Europeans. Although little of its ancient heritage remains, there is still plenty to see in modern Alexandria, Egypt's second largest city after Cairo *(see p95)*. *Map A1*

A Day Beside the Suez Canal in Port Said

Morning

Start your day near the green-domed **Suez Canal Authority Building** on the edge of the canal. From here, take a fun, free ride across the canal and back, courtesy of the car ferries that shuttle back and forth every 15 minutes between here and the far shore. Returning to where you started, head north along the canal on Sharia Filisteen, passing at No. 43 the Tourist Office (open 9am–2pm Sat–Thu), where you can pick up a good map. As you continue to walk northwards, look out for the faded façade of the Simon Artz department store and the imposing monolith of the lighthouse. Continue to the end of the pedestrian promenade, where you will encounter an empty sandstone plinth on which a statue of Ferdinand De Lesseps, French builder of the canal, once stood before it was hauled down after the 1952 Revolution. From here, hop in a taxi for a five-minute drive to **Al-Borg**, the best seafood restaurant in Egypt *(see p61)*.

Afternoon

Head inland to main Sharia 23rd July and follow it west. Stop at the small **Military Museum** (open 9am–3pm Sat–Thu), which has exhibits relating to the Arab-Israeli wars. Then cut diagonally across the main plaza and continue south to the town's bazaar, where, as well as cheap goods, you'll find many traditional Port Said buildings fronted by multi-storey wooden balconies.

Left **Step Pyramid** Right **Interior of the Mastaba of Ti**

TOP 10 Saqqara

1 Step Pyramid

The Step Pyramid, the first pyramid in Egypt, was built in the 27th century BC by the architect Imhotep for the 3rd-Dynasty King Djoser. It marks a leap forward in the history of world architecture. It is currently being restored.

2 Step Pyramid Court

This is a vast enclosure with a corridor of 40 columns and a reconstructed boundary wall, part of which bears a frieze of rearing cobras. On the north side, a stone box *(serdab)* contains a life-size statue of King Djoser.

3 Pyrmaid of Unas

Unas was the last king of the 5th Dynasty. His pyramid contains the earliest known examples of decorative writing. It is closed to the public but many of the tombs that line the causeway are open to visitors.

4 Persian Tombs

These are some of the deepest underground burial chambers in Egypt. They belong to three officials of the 27th Dynasty, which was founded by the Persians in 525 BC. The tomb walls bear colourful inscriptions.

5 Pyramid of Teti

The 6th-Dynasty pyramid has collapsed but the interior chambers can be visited. The walls are decorated with the earliest examples of ancient funerary writings accessible to the public.

6 Tomb of Mereruka

This is the tomb of King Teti's son-in-law. It has 33 chambers and some magnificent wall paintings, including a hunting scene in a marsh, as well as a life-size statute of Mereruka striding from a false door.

7 Tomb of Ankhma-Hor

This is also referred to as the "Physician's Tomb" because of its fascinating wall reliefs depicting surgical operations. These include surgery being performed on a man's toe and, apparently, a circumcision, as practised over 4,000 years ago.

8 Serapeum

A series of long, dark passageways house giant granite sarcophagi. Weighing up to 70 tonnes each, these once contained mummified corpses of bulls seen as an incarnation of Ptah, god of Memphis.

9 Mastaba of Ti

This is the tomb of a court official who served three kings during the 5th Dynasty. It has wall paintings that are unrivalled for the information they provide about life in ancient Egypt.

10 Imhotep Museum

This small museum has a short introductory film to the site, a large-scale model of the Step Pyramid complex as it originally was and some superb artefacts uncovered at Saqqara.

For general information about the site of Saqqara **see p91**

Left **Fort Qaitbey** Right **Roman amphitheatre at Kom al-Dikka**

Top 10 Alexandria

1 Biblioteca Alexandrina
This landmark library is worth visiting for its architecture, Antiquities Museum, Manuscript Museum and temporary exhibitions. *Map T2 • Corniche, Chatby • 03 483 9999 • Library open 11am–7pm Sat–Thu, 3–7pm Fri; Antiquities Museum open 9am–7pm Sun–Thu, 1–7pm Fri, 11am–7pm Sat • www.bibalex.org • Adm*

2 Fort Qaitbey
This pretty 15th-century fort sits on the site of the Pharos, which was a skyscraping lighthouse once regarded as one of the Seven Wonders of the Ancient World. *Map S1 • Eastern Harbour • Open 9am–5pm • Adm*

3 Graeco-Roman Museum
This museum contains about 40,000 items covering the history of Alexandria *(see p47).* *Map T2 • 5 Al-Mathaf al-Romani • 03 486 5820 • Closed for renovation until further notice • Adm*

4 Alexandria National Museum
One of Egypt's newest museums has well-displayed artifacts *(see p47).* *Map T2 • 110 Tariq al-Horreya • 03 483 5519 • Open 9am–4pm • www.alexmuseum.gov.eg • Adm*

5 Catacombs of Kom as-Shoqafa
This fascinating underground burial complex dating from the 2nd century AD has carved Medusa heads. *Map R3 • Sharia al-Nasseriya, Karmous • Open 9am–5pm • Adm*

6 Pompey's Pillar
All that is left of the Serapeum, Classical Alexandria's main temple complex (described as being second only to the Capitol in Rome), is this pillar of red Aswan granite, erected about AD 297. *Map R–S3 • Sharia Ahmed al-Sawari, Karmous • Open 9am–5pm • Adm*

7 Kom al-Dikka
This is an ancient hill that has been excavated to reveal a small semi-circular Roman theatre. On another part of the site are mosaics depicting birds. *Map S2 • Sharia Yousef • Open 9am–5pm • Adm*

8 Cavafy Museum
Constantine Cavafy (1863–1933) was a Greek Alexandrian poet of international renown. This museum is in the flat where he spent his last years. *Map S2 • 4 Sharia Sharm al-Sheikh, off Sharia Nabi Daniel • Open 10am–3pm Mon–Wed, Fri & Sat, 10am–5pm Thu & Sun • Adm*

9 Royal Jewellery Museum
A glittering array of treasures, including a platinum crown inlaid with over 2,000 diamonds, are on show in a villa that used to belong to Fatma Al-Zahraa. *21 Sharia Ahmed Yehia Pasha, Gleem • 03 582 8348 • Currently closed due to theft • Adm*

10 Midan Ramla
This square at the heart of Alexandria is ringed by splendid early 20th-century institutions, notably the Trianon patisserie and tearoom. *Map S2*

For general information about the city of Alexandria **see p93**

The mortuary temple of Ramses II, the Ramesseum

Luxor

DESPITE THE LARGE NUMBERS OF TOURISTS IT ATTRACTS, *Luxor is little more than a small town on the banks of the Nile. Hundreds of thousands of international visitors flock here to marvel at what the modern town was built upon, which is the spectacular ruins of Thebes, vast capital of the pharaohs during the New Kingdom (1550–1069 BC). Only two temples remain – Luxor Temple in the heart of the town and the Karnak temple complex just north of the town. Both were renowned throughout the ancient world and have attracted visitors ever since ancient Greek and Roman times. Even more extraordinary are the sites on the West Bank, which is where the pharaohs built their grand funerary temples and tombs. Cross by ferry, or over the road bridge located 7 km (4 miles) south of the town centre. Tickets for these monuments need to be bought in advance from a ticket office on the West Bank.*

The Colossi of Memnon

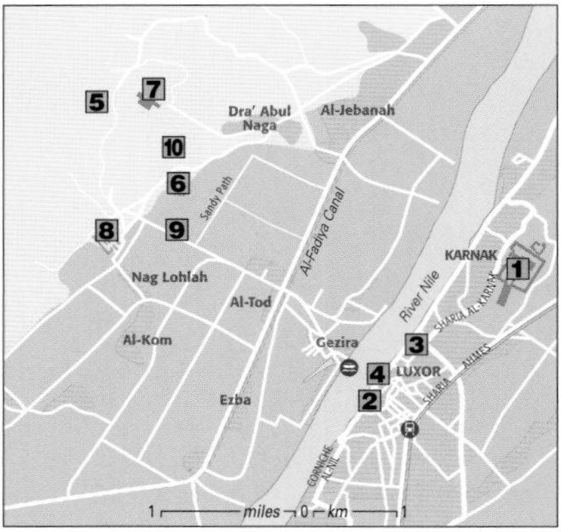

Top 10 Sights

1. Karnak
2. Luxor Temple
3. Luxor Museum
4. Mummification Museum
5. Valley of the Kings
6. Ramesseum
7. Temple of Hatshepsut
8. Medinat Habu
9. Colossi of Memnon
10. Tombs of the Nobles

Preceding pages **View of Aswan and the Nile**

Hypostyle Hall in the Temple of Amun, Karnak

1 Karnak

The greatest of all Egypt's ancient monuments is this vast complex of multiple temples, courts and shrines. Karnak was a political, religious and military powerbase, home to the pharaoh, the high priests and an enormous corps of administrators. Pharaohs from the 12th to the 22nd Dynasty ruled from here, including Ramses II and Tutankhamun, and most of them left their mark in some way. There is so much to see that it is worth visiting both by day and again by night for the Sound and Light Show *(see pp16–17)*.

2 Luxor Temple

The modern town has grown up around this temple, which occupies a prime, central spot beside the Nile. It exerts a commanding presence, acting as a constant reminder of how much in thrall to the pharaohs the modern town remains. Majestic by day, the temple takes on an unearthly quality by night when precision flood lighting adds drama to the huge stone figures and the carved reliefs that cover most surfaces *(see pp20–21)*.

Colossus of Ramses II, Luxor Temple

3 Luxor Museum

Situated on the Corniche halfway between Luxor Temple and Karnak, this modern, purpose- built museum exhibits an excellent collection of statuary and artefacts, almost all of which were found in tombs and temples in the Luxor area. Unlike many other museums in Egypt, the presentation is world-class, with pieces well lit and informatively labelled in multiple languages, including English. A visit here will greatly enhance your appreciation of Luxor's many monuments *(see p47)*. For a description of the museum's best items, see p102. *Map Z1 • Corniche al-Nil, East Bank • 095 238 0269 • Open 9am–5pm • Adm*

4 Mummification Museum

Although not large, this museum manages within a relatively compact space to explain not only the methods of mummification – occasionally in quite alarming detail – but also the reasons for it. Choice ancient artefacts illustrate the texts, including materials and tools used in the mummification process. The symbols and icons of the afterlife are also clearly explained via pictorial boards. There are also plenty of intriguing, fun exhibits, including a mummified cat and ram, a cross-section of a mummified skull stuffed with material where the brain has been removed and a piece of a mummified toe *(see p47)*. *Map Y2 • Corniche al-Nil, East Bank • 095 238 1501 • Open 9am–2pm, 5–9pm in summer; 9am–2pm, 4–9pm in winter • Adm*

The impressive mortuary temple of Ramses III, Medinat Habu

5 Valley of the Kings

By digging their tombs deep into the Theban Hills the pharaohs hoped to stop robbers stealing the priceless possessions buried with them. It was an unsuccessful strategy. Every burial chamber discovered to date had been raided except for those of Yuya and Thuya and Tutankhamun *(see p40–41)*. The vacant tombs are fascinating, with the corridor walls and burial chambers stunningly adorned with painted reliefs designed to help the pharaoh navigate the Underworld *(see pp24–5)*.

6 Ramesseum

Ramses II was ruler of Egypt for 67 years and he built his mortuary temple as a statement of his eternal greatness. The huge complex dedicated to Amun, which took almost 20 years to build, now lies mostly in ruins with only some columns still standing *(see p38)*. *Map V3 • 1 km (0.6 miles) NE of West Bank ticket office • Open 6am–5pm • Adm*

Crossing the Nile

Since the opening of the Luxor Bridge in 1998, 7 km (4 miles) south of town, all coaches, cars and taxis use this route to get from Luxor to the West Bank. For pedestrians and cyclists there's a frequent local ferry (£E1), or you can hire a motorboat or felucca for around £E15–20.

7 Temple of Hatshepsut

Against its stark mountainous backdrop, the partly rock-hewn Mortuary Temple of Hatshepsut is an awe-inspiring sight and one of the most popular monuments on the West Bank. It was designed by Queen Hatshepsut's architect Senenmut in the 18th Dynasty. The temple was damaged by Ramses II and his successors, and Christians later turned it into a monastery (hence its alternative name, Deir al-Bahri, which means "Northern Monastery"). Ongoing restorations of the site have done much to revive former glories and have revealed some exquisite decoration *(see pp22–3)*.

8 Medinat Habu

It is a great mystery why this magnificent mortuary temple raised by Ramses III is not visited more. It is second in size only to Karnak, and is in a far more complete state than the nearby Ramesseum, on which Medinat Habu is modelled. Ramses III's military campaigns are recorded in detail on the main entrance pylon and on the walls inside. In the second court, colourful reliefs are well preserved thanks to early Christians, who converted a part of the temple into a church and covered the offending images with plaster *(see p38)*. *Map U4 • W of West Bank ticket office • Open 6am–5pm • Adm*

9 Colossi of Memnon

Standing in a field beside the road that runs from the Nile to the Theban Hills, these two lone colossi are the first things most visitors see on arriving at the West Bank. They represent Amenhotep III and are all that is left of the pharaoh's mortuary temple, thought to have been the largest ever built in Egypt. The temple was gradually destroyed by the annual floods of the Nile and plundered for building material by later pharaohs.

Map V3 • 1 km (0.6 mile) E of West Bank ticket office

10 Tombs of the Nobles

These are the tombs of the administrators and high officials of the New Kingdom. In contrast to the royal tombs hidden in the Valley of the Kings, the nobles' tombs were built close to the surface and were open to descendents to visit and leave offerings. Vivid artworks cover their walls, providing an insight into daily life in ancient Egypt. The tombs are divided into six groups, each of which requires its own ticket. For information on specific tombs, see p103.

Map V3 • W of West Bank ticket office, follow signposts for Sheikh Abd al-Gurna Tombs • Open 6am–5pm • Adm

Tomb of Sennefer, Tombs of the Nobles

A Stroll Along the Corniche

Morning

Start the day with breakfast at the Metropolitan Café on the lower level of the Corniche by Luxor Temple. It has great views across the Nile. The morning is a good time to visit **Luxor Temple** *(see pp20–21)*, before the heat gets too overwhelming. Afterwards, continue north up the Corniche, turning right onto Sharia al-Montazah; here you have a view of the **Avenue of Sphinxes** *(see p20)* that connects Luxor Temple with Karnak. It is also possible to see how parts of the modern town are being removed to reveal the avenue beneath. Continue north up the Corniche, stopping for a visit to the **Mummification Museum** *(see p99)*, then passing a couple of run-down colonial-era buildings on your right, one of which was one of the earliest hotels in town and now houses the city council. Stop for lunch at **Kebabgy** on the Corniche *(see p106)*.

Afternoon

Just a short walk further north on the Corniche is the **Luxor Museum** *(see p99)* with its superb collection of artefacts from various tombs and temples. Afterwards, instead of walking all the way back, take a calèche, one of the horse-drawn carriages that patrol the town. The official rate is £E30 per hour, but the drivers usually charge more. Ask the driver to take you back to the **Winter Palace Hotel** *(see p129)* for a late afternoon drink on the front terrace.

Left **A relief on the Talatat Wall** Right **Detail of the statue of Sobek enthroned with Amenhotep III**

TOP 10 Luxor Museum

1 Head of Amenhotep III
Displayed near the museum entrance is this massive pharaoh's head in granite, originally part of Amenhotep's immense mortuary temple, of which nothing survives except the Colossi of Memnon *(see p101)*.

2 Golden Cow Head
Also near the entrance is a gilded head representing Mehit-Weret, an aspect of Hathor, cow-headed goddess of love. It is carved from wood, with copper horns and eyes of lapis lazuli, and was discovered in the tomb of Tutankhamun.

3 Cachette Hall
This hall contains 16 of the statues found beneath Luxor Temple in 1989, including a statue of Amenhotep III, who largely built the temple. The statue is one of the finest pieces of ancient Egyptian art.

4 Horemheb and Atum
Also notable in the Cachette Hall is the unusual paired statue depicting King Horemheb kneeling before Atum, who is sitting on his throne and measures almost 2 m (6.5 ft) in height.

5 Statue of Sobek
This beautifully expressive statue depicts the crocodile-god Sobek with his arm draped paternally around the shoulders of the young Pharaoh Amenhotep III.

6 The Glory of Thebes Hall
This hall is devoted to the military history of ancient Egypt. Exhibits include ancient weapons, reliefs depicting battle scenes and Tutankhamun's hunting chariot.

7 Royal Mummies
Also in the Glory of Thebes Hall are two royal mummies of Ahmose, the pharaoh who drove the Hyksos out of Egypt and reunited the country, starting the golden New Kingdom era. There is also a mummy of what might be Ramses I.

8 Tutankhamun Treasures
On the first floor, glass cabinets display items from Tutankhamun's tomb, including sandals, arrow heads, two solar barques and several gilded *shabti* (small figures placed in the tomb to help the pharaoh in the afterlife).

9 Akhenaten
A couple of eerie heads from large Osiride statues of the heretic Pharaoh Akhenaten (Amenhotep IV) are also on the first floor. They are from the Aten Temple at Karnak.

10 Talatat Wall
This is a reassembled wall of 283 painted sandstone blocks from the Aten Temple at Karnak. It has reliefs depicting scenes of daily life during the time of Akhenaten, all executed in the hyper-stylized fashion peculiar to the king's reign.

For more information on the Luxor Museum, including opening times, **see p99**

Left **Wall painting in the Tomb of Sennefer** Right **Wall painting in the Tomb of Nakht**

Top 10 Tombs of the Nobles

1 Tomb of Sennefer
Sennefer was mayor of Thebes and overseer of the gardens at Amun under Amenhotep III. His is one of the best preserved tombs, with a ceiling covered with brightly coloured paintings of vines.

2 Tomb of Rekhmire
Rekhmire was a vizier under Tuthmosis III and Amenhotep II and his tomb depicts him collecting taxes and receiving gifts from foreign lands. Among the tributes shown are vases from Crete and a giraffe and monkeys from Punt (present day Somalia).

3 Tomb of Nakht
This tomb is decorated with scenes of rural life, such as fishing, hunting and harvesting, as well as a banqueting scene with dancers and a harpist. It is one of the most fascinating tombs with exceptionally vivid and lively paintings.

4 Tomb of Menna
Menna was an inspector of estates. Paintings in his tomb depict him and his wife making offerings to the gods. A scene in the inner chamber also portrays him hunting and fishing.

5 Tomb of Userhat
Userhat was one of Amenhotep II's scribes. His tomb has detailed scenes of everyday life, including a trip to the barbers.

6 Tomb of Ramose
Ramose was a governor of Thebes around the time of Akhenaten's Amarna revolution, when the pharaoh overthrew Egyptian polytheism in favour of the worship of a single god, Aten. This superb tomb is interesting for featuring both Classical and Amarna-style reliefs.

7 Tomb of Khonsu
Khonsu was an advisor to Tuthmosis III. His tomb is painted with colourful scenes depicting the Festival of Montu.

8 Tomb of Benia
Benia was a supervisor of construction work. As with the other two tombs in this group, Benia's tomb has paintings depicting vignettes of life, as well as statues of the deceased and both his parents.

9 Khokha Tombs
This trio of tombs was built for New Kingdom officials. Discovered in 1915, they were opened to the public only in 1995. Their decoration is similar to the other tombs in this area.

10 Assasif Tombs
These are three more tombs that lie between the main Tombs of the Nobles and the Temple of Hatshepsut. Some of the Assasif tombs date from the Late Period, notably the Tomb of Pabasa, which has detailed bee-keeping and fruit-picking scenes.

For general information about the Tombs of the Nobles and details of opening times and admission prices **see p101**

Left **The ruins of the village of Deir al-Medina** Right **Tomb wall painting, Valley of the Queens**

TOP 10 Best of the Rest

1 Deir al-Medina
The labourers who built the royal tombs lived here. Several of their tombs and a small Ptolemaic temple can be visited. *Map U3 • 1 km (0.6 mile) NW of West Bank ticket office • Open 6am–5pm • Adm*

2 Valley of the Queens
This holds the tombs of many royal wives and children. Although there are nearly 80 tombs, only a few are open to the public. *Map U3 • 1 km (0.6 mile) NW of West Bank ticket office • Open 6am–5pm • Adm*

3 Tomb of Nefertari
The tomb of the favourite wife of Ramses the Great has the most complete paintings of all the tombs, but they are very fragile. *Map U3 • Valley of the Queens, 1 km (0.6 mile) NW of West Bank ticket office • Closed to the public*

4 Temple of Seti I
This temple is ruinous, but it has some interesting reliefs. *Map X3 • 3 km (2 miles) E of West Bank ticket office • Adm*

5 Howard Carter's House
The home of the man who discovered Tutankhamun's tomb shows a 3D film on the excavation. *Map X2 • 3 km (2 miles) E of West Bank ticket office • Open 6am–6pm (until 5pm in winter) • Adm*

6 Temple of Merneptah
The reconstructed remains of this mortuary temple are next to the Ramesseum. *Map V3 • 1 km (0.6 mile) NE of West Bank ticket office • Open 6am–5pm • Adm*

7 Tomb of Ay
Ay was Tutankhamun's successor and his fine tomb has both royal and noble imagery. *Map U2 • Western Valley • Open 6am–5pm • Adm*

8 The Donkey Trail
Starting near the Tomb of Ramses I in the Valley of the Kings is a scenic trail that leads to the Temple of Hatshepsut. The hike takes about 30 minutes, but beware the heat in summer. *Map V2 • 2 km (1 mile) N of West Bank ticket office*

9 West Bank Villages
Spend some time in these sleepy, pretty villages. They may be demolished in the near future. *Map X5*

10 New Gurna
Completed in 1948, New Gurna was built as an attempt to rehouse Gurna residents away from the antiquities, but it is now falling into disrepair. *Map W4*

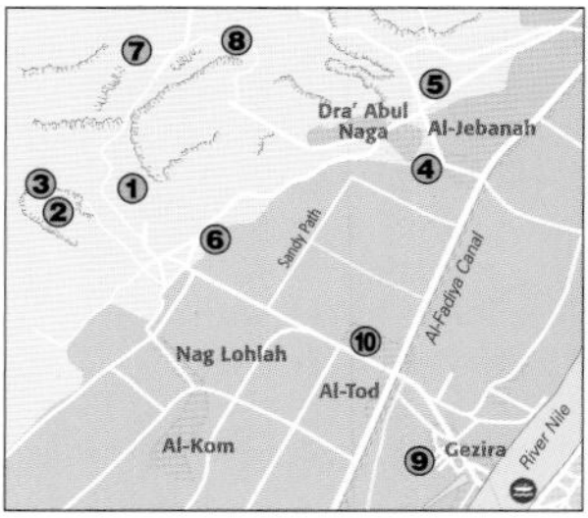

Left **Feluccas on the Nile** Right **Hot-air ballooning**

Top 10 Outdoor Activities

1 Hot-Air Ballooning
Several companies offer hot-air balloon excursions over Luxor. Weather permitting, they leave at dawn from sites on the West Bank and flights last about 30–40 minutes. They can be booked through your hotel.

2 Seaplane Flights
An even higher view of Luxor can be enjoyed from the comfort of a small seaplane. Departures (every morning) are from a jetty near Karnak and the flight lasts about 30 minutes. You can book through your hotel.

3 Cycling
Cycling is a great way to get around the West Bank. You can hire bikes on Sharia al-Mahatta and Sharia Televizyun in Luxor town, and then take them across the river on the ferry, or hire them from the village by the ferry on the West Bank. *Map V2*

4 Felucca Trips
A popular felucca trip is to sail to Banana Island (Geziret al-Moz), where you can stroll through the banana groves. A round trip takes two to three hours. *Map W6*

5 Bird-Watching
Crocodile Island is excellent for bird-watching. There are at least 50 species of bird here. You can get a bus to the island from the Winter Palace hotel *(see p129)*. *Map W6 • Crocodile Island, 4 km (2.5 miles S of Luxor town)*

6 Swimming
The El-Luxor hotel *(see p129)* allows non-residents to use its pools for a day fee. It is not safe to swim in the Nile.

7 Golf
Luxor has an 18-hole, par 72 course at the Royal Valley Golf Club. Daily memberships are offered, and the club has caddies, club rental and power carts. Many of the big hotels provide special golf packages. *Map Z6 • 13 km (9 miles) from Luxor town, E Bank • 095 928 0098 • www.golfluxor.com*

8 Horse-Riding
Horses can be hired by the hour from stables in Gezira, the small village next to the ferry landing on the West Bank. Ask for the Pharaoh's Stables or Arabian Horse Stables, or book in advance through your hotel. *Map W6 • Arabian Horse Stables: 095 231 0024 • Pharaoh's Stables: 095 231 2263*

9 Caleche Rides
A horse-drawn carriage ride around town is pleasant at any time of day. Haggle hard, and agree in advance a price for the ride, not per person.

10 Sunbathing
Egypt is a traditional Muslim country, where displays of flesh will offend locals (and, in the case of improperly dressed women, invite sexual harassment). Confine sunbathing to your hotel pool.

Price Categories

For a two-course meal for one with a soft drink and including service

£	under £E30
££	£E30–£60
£££	£E60–£120
££££	£E120–£250
£££££	over £E250

Above **Kebabgy**

TOP 10 Restaurants and Cafés

1 1886 Restaurant, Winter Palace

This upmarket French restaurant requires reservations and formal dress (jacket and tie for men) *(see p61)*. *Map Y2–3 • Winter Palace, Corniche al-Nil, East Bank • 095 2380 422 • Closed lunch • ££££*

2 Kebabgy

Popular for snacks (including pizza and pasta), this waterside restaurant also serves grilled meats. *Map Y2 • Corniche al-Nil, East Bank • £££*

3 La Mamma, Sheraton

The best Italian food in town is served here on a terrace *(see p129)*. *Map X6 • Sheraton Luxor Resort, Sharia Khaled Ibn al-Walid, Awamiya, East Bank • 095 227 4544 • £££*

4 Sofra

This simple but charming restaurant serves Mediterranean-influenced Egyptian dishes. *Map Z3 • 90 Sharia Mohammed Farid, East Bank • 095 235 9752 • £££*

5 La Corniche, Winter Palace

The larger of this hotel's eateries has a broader, more international menu than the 1886. *Map Y2–3 • Winter Palace, Corniche al-Nil, East Bank • 095 2380 422 • Closed lunch • ££££*

6 The Lantern

Owned by an Anglo-Egyptian couple (as reflected in the menu, which includes both *shish tawouk* and chicken curry), this restaurant is popular with local expats. *Map X6 • Sharia al-Roda al-Sharifa, off Khaled Ibn al-Walid, East Bank • 095 236 1451 • £££*

7 Tutankhamun

This small local restaurant near the ferry landing beside the river has a great view across to the Luxor Temple. *Map X5 • Al-Gezira, West Bank • 0100 566 8614 • £££*

8 King's Head Pub

A favourite with the town's UK visitors, this is a restaurant-pub. *Map X6 • Sharia Khalid Ibn al-Walid, East Bank • 095 228 0489 • £££*

9 El-Gezira

This rooftop restaurant with great Nile views serves Egyptian specialities *(see p130)*. *Map X5 • El-Gezira, West Bank • 095 231 0034 • ££*

10 Al-Moudira

This hotel serves lunch in its Swimming Pool Pavilion and dinner in the Great Room, which has a Mediterranean-inspired menu *(see p129)*. *Map X2 • Haggar Daba'iyya, West Bank • 012 325 1307 • ££££*

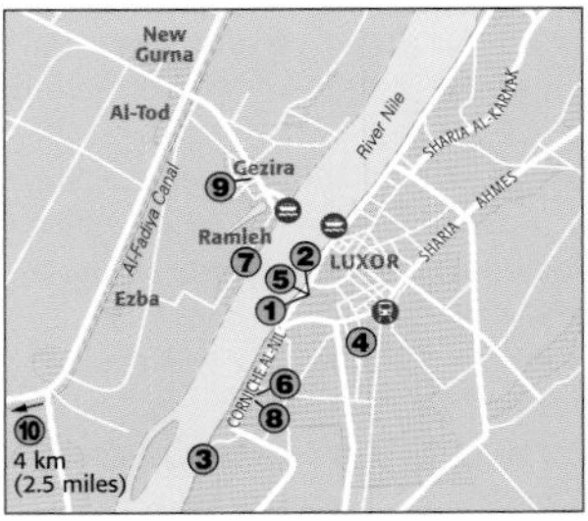

Recommend your favourite restaurant or café on **traveldk.com**

Left **Granite falcon (Horus), Temple of Horus, Edfu** Right **Carved wall, Temple of Hathor, Dendara**

TOP 10 Around Luxor

1 Tell al-Amarna

Few independent tourists get to this remote site to see the ruins of the city built by pharaoh Akhenaten and his wife Nefertiti. *Map B3 • Al-Minya Governorate, 12 km (7 miles) SW of Mallawi • Open 7am–5pm (last adm: 4pm) • Adm*

2 Abydos

The cult centre of Osiris, Abydos was the holiest of places in Pharaonic times. The remains include the Temple of Seti I *(see p38)*. *Map B4 • 150 km (90 miles) NW of Luxor • Open 8am–5pm • Adm*

3 Dendara

Just outside Qena is a well-preserved, large Graeco-Roman temple dedicated to Hathor. It is one of the most intact temples in Egypt *(see p39)*. *Map B4 • 60 km (37 miles) N of Luxor • Open 7am–6pm in summer, 7am–5pm in winter • Adm*

4 Western Desert

This lies between the Nile Valley and the border with Libya. Tourist agencies run day trips to the sands of the White Desert – make enquiries at your hotel.

5 Esna

This small market town is best known for the remains of the Temple of Khnum, of which only the hypostyle hall has been excavated. The site is visited on the return leg (Aswan–Luxor) of most Nile cruises. *Map B5 • 54 km (33 miles) S of Luxor • Open 7am–8pm in summer, 7am–5pm in winter • Adm*

6 Edfu

Halfway between Luxor and Aswan, Edfu is the first stop on most Nile cruises for the Temple of Horus, the largest and best preserved Graeco-Roman temple in Egypt *(see p38)*. *Map C5 • 115 km (71 miles) S of Luxor • Open 6am–8pm in summer, 7am–6pm in winter • Adm*

7 Al-Kab

This was once the ancient city of Nekheb, dedicated to the vulture goddess, Nekhbet. Little remains today except for four tombs of ancient nobles. *Map C5 • 15 km (9 miles) S of Edfu • Open 8am–5pm • Adm*

8 Silsilah

On the banks of the Nile between Edfu and Kom Ombo are ancient quarries cut into rocky cliff faces. Feluccas sailing from Aswan often stop here to let passengers view ancient graffiti. *Map C5 • 35 km (22 miles) S of Edfu*

9 Kom Ombo

Overlooking the Nile, this is a dual temple on a symmetrical plan, jointly dedicated to the falcon god Horus and crocodile god Sobek. *Map C5 • 40 km (25 miles) N of Aswan • Open 7am–9pm in summer, 7am–7pm in winter • Adm*

10 Daraw

This small town hosts a famous Tuesday camel market, with animals from Sudan. *Map C5 • 32 km (20 miles) N of Aswan • Open 7am–2pm Tue*

Left **Nubia Museum** Right **Tombs of the Nobles**

Aswan and Lake Nasser

EGYPT'S SOUTHERNMOST CITY WAS AN IMPORTANT *garrison town guarding the frontier in ancient times. It has also always been a major trading post for goods arriving from Africa. Even today the town feels more "African" than Middle Eastern, in part due to the darker skin of many of its inhabitants, who are Nubians rather than Arabs. Life here moves at a languid pace and the sightseeing is less frenetic than in Luxor. The Nile is also particularly beautiful here, dotted with islands and with a west bank of sandy, desert slopes that come right down to the water's edge. Aswan is gateway to Lake Nasser* (see p113), *the vast reservoir that stretches about 500 km (300 miles) behind the High Dam, south into neighbouring Sudan.*

Elephantine Island

Top 10 Sights

1. **Souq**
2. **Nubia Museum**
3. **Elephantine Island**
4. **Kitchener's Island**
5. **Felucca Rides**
6. **Tombs of the Nobles**
7. **Unfinished Obelisk**
8. **Temple of Philae**
9. **High Dam**
10. **Abu Simbel**

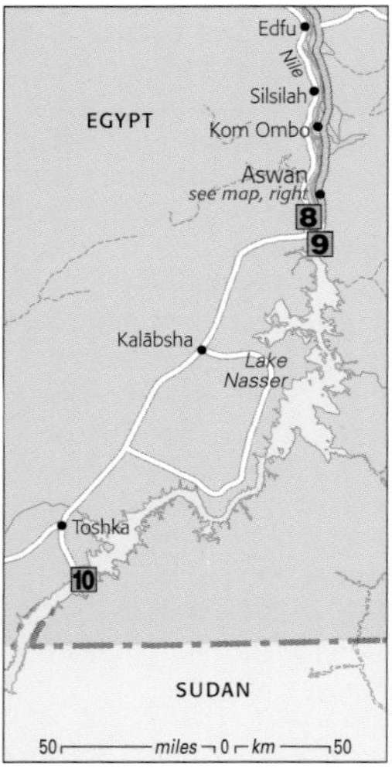

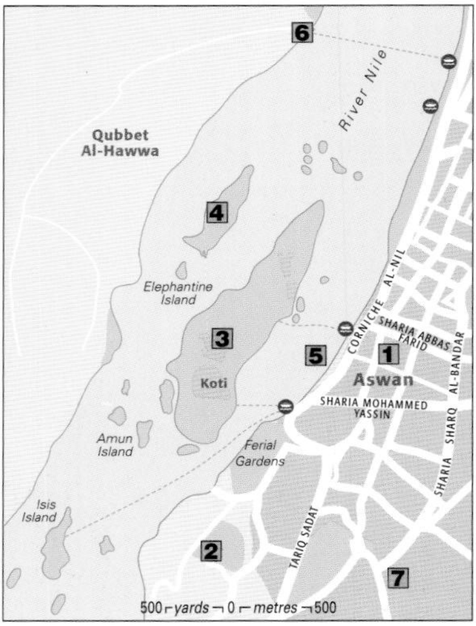

Aswan souq

1 Souq

Filling one long street (Sharia al-Souq) that runs parallel to the riverside Corniche, Aswan's souq is the best in Egypt outside of Cairo. It is especially good for spices and dyes. Look out for dried hibiscus, boiled to make the drink *karkade*. You can also buy Nubian jewellery, scarves, skull-caps, embroidered *galabiyyas* and baskets. As in Cairo, it's important that you haggle, or face paying way over the odds. *Map T4–5*

2 Nubia Museum

Nubia is the area between Aswan in Egypt and Khartoum in Sudan. This museum has displays on Nubian life from the earliest settlements to the modern day. It also has a garden with a typical distinctive Nubian house, and a water feature showing the Nile's course and cataracts *(see p47)*. *Map S6 • Sharia al-Fanadek • 097 231 9222 • Open 9am–1pm, 6–10pm (summer); 9am–1pm, 5–9pm (winter) • www.numibia.net/nubia • Adm*

3 Elephantine Island

The largest of the islands at Aswan, Elephantine Island is also the site of the town's oldest settlement. In ancient times it was the cult centre of the ram-headed god of the Nile flood, Khnum. Among the ruins at the southern end are those of the Temple of Khnum, built by Nectanebo in the 4th century BC. Regular ferries connect the island with the Corniche. *Map S5–6*

4 Kitchener's Island

Behind Elephantine Island is the much smaller Kitchener's Island, named after the British general Horatio Kitchener, who was presented with the island in the 1890s as a reward for leading the Egyptian army's successful campaigns in Sudan. Kitchener, a keen botanist, planted the island with exotic plants and flowers from all over the world. To get to it you need to hire a felucca and ask the captain either to wait or to return for you at an agreed time. *Map S5 • Open 7am–sunset • Adm*

Kitchener's Island

A felucca sailing past the Tombs of the Nobles

5 Felucca Rides

Aswan is the finest place to go sailing in a felucca. You can hire one by the hour or for the day and use it as your personal transport to visit Elephantine and Kitchener's islands and the tombs on the west bank. The more adventurous might consider a two-night, three-day cruise to Edfu. The boats take up to six people and conditions are basic. The felucca captains congregate on the Corniche. Alternatively, you can have your hotel make the arrangements, or ask the tourist office for advice.

6 Tombs of the Nobles

The hills on the west bank of the Nile at Aswan have tombs hewn out of the rock dating from the Old and Middle Kingdoms. The best (No.31) is that of Prince Sarenput II, governor of southern Egypt during the 12th Dynasty. It is decorated with statues of the prince and painted scenes of hunting and fishing. To get to the tombs take a local ferry from the Corniche near the railway station. *Map S4 • Qubbet al-Hawa, West Bank • Open 7am–5pm • Adm*

7 Unfinished Obelisk

One of the strangest sites in Egypt is a huge obelisk still attached to the bedrock in an ancient quarry in the hills south of Aswan that supplied the ancient Egyptians with red granite for their temples and statues. Three sides of the shaft were completed before a flaw was discovered in the stone and the obelisk was abandoned. Had it been completed, it would have weighed an astonishing 1.8 million kg (1,197 tons) and stood 41 m (134 ft) high. *Map T6 • 1.5 km (1 mile) S of Aswan • Open 7am–5pm • Adm*

8 Temple of Philae

A highlight of Aswan, and reason alone to pay a visit to the town, is this Graeco-Roman temple dedicated to the cult of Isis. It is situated on its own picturesque island in the middle of the Nile and the only way to visit it is by motor launch, which makes for a supremely dramatic approach. It lies between the Aswan and High Dams, a 15-minute drive south of town, and is usually visited as part of an organized tour, although it is possible to get a taxi – just ask for Shallal, which is where the motorboats dock *(see pp28–9)*.

Dam

Egypt's fortunes have historically always been linked to the annual flooding of the Nile. In order to regulate this the British built the Aswan Dam between 1898 and 1902. This soon proved too small to control the river's unpredictable floods and in the 1960s President Nasser began construction of the High Dam. The resultant increases in agricultural production and hydroelectricity have saved Egypt from famine.

9 High Dam

Built between 1960 and 1971, the enormous High Dam is 3,830 m (12,562 ft) across, 111 m (364 ft) high and 980 m (3,214 ft) wide at its base. At the eastern end of the dam there is a visitors' pavilion detailing the construction of the dam and at the western end there is a lotus-shaped tower, built to commemorate the Soviet Union's assistance in the project, that also has an observation deck. The dam is usually visited as part of tours to Abu Simbel. *Map C5 • 17 km (11 miles) S of Aswan • Open 7am–5pm*

The Sun Temple at Abu Simbel

10 Abu Simbel

Hewn out of a solid cliff in the 13th century BC, the great Sun Temple and the smaller Temple of Hathor at Abu Simbel are a breathtaking sight. Although dedicated to the gods, the Sun Temple is really a monument to the pharaoh Ramses II, as a statement of his power. His image dominates the façade in the form of four seated colossi. The temple is usually visited as a day trip from Aswan, a convoy of vehicles departing early in the morning and returning late in the afternoon. Abu Simbel also has its own airport *(see pp30–31)*.

A Day in Aswan

Morning

Aswan is not a great sightseeing city like Cairo or Luxor. It is a mellow town, partly because the heat slows down the tempo. Start the day with breakfast on your boat before going ashore. Then head inland until you come to Sharia al-Souk, and walk south. In recent years the **souq** has been smartened up and part of it has been converted into a pedestrian-only promenade, but it remains authentic and is the most charming bazaar in Egypt. For a unique souvenir look out for local Nubian handicrafts and CDs of Nubian music. Eventually the souq peters out and Sharia al-Souq swings right to connect with the Corniche. Just north of here are a string of moored boats that double as restaurants, with the Aswan Moon *(Corniche al-Nil • 097 231 6108)* being a great spot to stop off for lunch.

Afternoon

The best way to combat the afternoon heat is to take to the water in a **felucca**. Boat captains tout for business on the Corniche and charge by the hour. You can choose to drift languidly or be dropped off on **Kitchener's Island** or on **Elephantine Island** *(see p109)* for further exploring. Later on, hire a felucca or catch the local ferry from near the **Aswan Museum** *(see p112)* on Elephantine Island back to the mainland and head to the nearby **Old Cataract Hotel** *(see p131)* for sundowners on the terrace. At dusk the river takes on a pink hue, which is beautiful and calming.

Left **Aswan Dam** Centre **Aga Khan Mausoleum** Right **A Nubian village, Elephantine Island**

TOP 10 Best of the Rest

1 Aga Khan Mausoleum
The Aga Khan III (1877–1957), leader of the Ismaili sect of Shiia Muslims, is buried in this private, Fatimid-style tomb atop a hillside. *Map R5 • West Bank • Closed to the public*

2 Monastery of St Simeon
This 7th-century monastery was abandoned after an attack in the 12th century. Its ruins are a 30-minute desert hike from the river's edge. *Map R5 • West Bank • Open 8am–4pm • Adm*

3 Aswan Museum
This museum houses artefacts found in and around Aswan and Elephantine Island – from prehistoric weapons to Graeco-Roman mummies. *Map S6 • Elephantine Island • Open 8am–4pm • Adm*

4 Nilometer
The walls of the square shaft of 90 rock-cut steps descending to the river are marked to record the height of the annual flood. This helps predict the likely crop yield for the coming year. *Map S6 • Elephantine Island • Adm included in ticket for Aswan Museum*

5 Old Cataract Hotel
This Moorish-styled hotel, with a lovely verandah overlooking the Nile, has been exquisitely renovated *(see pp53 & 131)*.

6 Issa Island
Issa Island is home to the Nubian Restaurant, which has a lovely garden. It is reached by free motorboat from near the Egypt Air office. *Map S6 • Issa Island • 097 910 8000*

7 Nubian House
This café/restaurant high on a hilltop overlooking the Nile serves Nubian food, but most people come for the magnificent views. *Map S6 • On the hill behind the Basma Hotel • 097 232 6226*

8 Fatimid Cemetery
This large dusty expanse is dotted with hundreds of mud-brick tombs, many of which date back to the 9th and 10th centuries. *Map S6 • Between the Nubian Museum and the Unfinished Obelisk*

9 Sehel Island
A felucca trip to this island, 4 km (2.5 miles) from Aswan, is a popular half-day excursion, not so much for anything that's there, but more for the pleasure of sailing the Nile. *Map R6 • Adm*

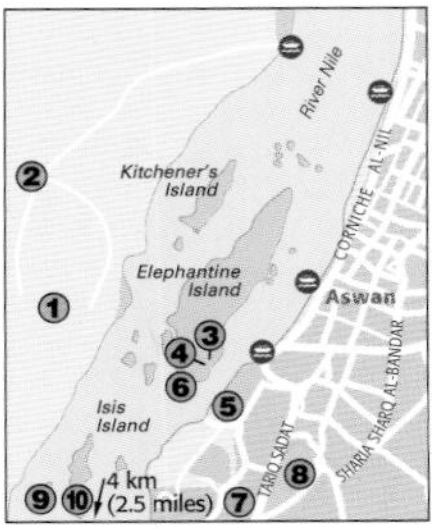

10 Aswan Dam
At the time of its construction (1898–1902), this British-built dam was the largest in the world. It was superseded in the 1970s by the High Dam. *Map B6 • 11 km (7 miles) S of Aswan • Adm*

Left **Temple of Kalabsha** Right **Pharaonic relief inside the Temple of Kalabsha**

TOP 10 Lake Nasser

1 Temple of Kalabsha

This striking temple was built by Emperor Augustus in the 1st century AD on the site of earlier buildings. It was moved north of its original location when Lake Nasser was created. *Map B5 • Just W of the High Dam • Open 7am–5pm in summer, 7am–4pm in winter • Adm*

2 Kiosk of Qertassi

The remains of this Roman-era pavillion beside Kalabsha Temple have two fine Hathor-headed columns at the entrance. *Map B5 • W of High Dam • Adm included in the ticket for Kalabsha Temple*

3 Wadi al-Sebua

This small temple was built by Ramses II. Approached by a half-buried avenue of sphinxes, it has colossi of the pharaoh. *Map B6 • 140 km (87 miles) S of High Dam*

4 Temple of Amada

Dedicated to Amun-Ra and Ra-Harakhty, Amada was built during the reigns of Tuthmosis III and Amenhotep II. It has some well-preserved reliefs. *Map B6 • 185 km (115 miles) S of High Dam*

5 Qasr Ibrim

Although dating back to 1000 BC, the main surviving structure in this fort are the ruins of an 8th-century cathedral. *Map B6 • 60 km (37 miles) N of Abu Simbel*

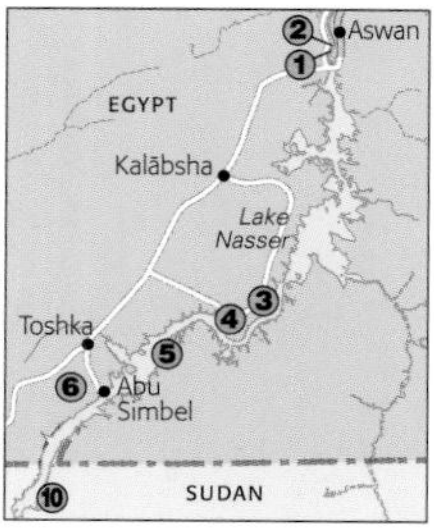

6 Abu Simbel

The imposing Sun Temple was built by Ramses II at the height of the New Kingdom era and is one of the most impressive ancient sites in Egypt *(see pp30–31)*.

7 Lake Nasser Cruises

Cruises on Lake Nasser take three days to sail from near the High Dam to Abu Simbel, calling at Wadi al-Sebua, Amada Temple and Qasr Ibrim *(see p133)*.

8 Crocodiles

Once common in Egypt, and worshipped in ancient times, crocodiles were hunted to extinction by the 1950s. However, in recent years they have returned in large numbers to Lake Nasser where they now thrive.

9 Angling

Lake Nasser is renowned for its fish stocks, particularly Nile perch, which grow here to monster dimensions. Several companies organize big game freshwater angling expeditions, notably African Angler. *www.african-angler.net*

10 Wadi Halfa

There is a weekly ferry from the High Dam that takes 24 hours to cruise the whole length of Lake Nasser to Wadi Halfa in Sudan. You will need a Sudanese visa.

STREETSMART

Left **Tourist office** Centre **Internet café** Right **Covering up in the sun**

TOP 10 Planning Your Trip

1 Internet Information

The following websites can help you research which parts of this fascinating country you want to cover during your visit. They also provide background information on ancient Egyptian history and Egyptology. *www.touregypt.net • www.sis.gov.eg/En • http://amun-ra-egyptology.blogspot.in • www.egypt.travel*

2 Climate

Avoid July and August, which are unbearably hot, with temperatures at a constant of around 30–40°C (85–105°F). The best weather is December to February, when the temperatures in Upper Egypt are much less uncomfortable, and, in Cairo, it can even get chilly in the evenings, making a jacket necessary.

3 When to Go

As far as temperature goes, winter is the best time of year, although hotels and cruises get booked up over Christmas and New Year. November and late January/February are good for avoiding the worst of the crowds. You may also want to steer clear of the holy month of Ramadan *(see p62)*, when opening hours are erratic.

4 Visas

Most nationalities require a tourist visa to enter Egypt. These can be secured in advance from Egyptian consulates in your own country but it is much easier and cheaper to obtain them on arrival at Cairo or Luxor airport; this takes just a few minutes and costs the equivalent of US $15 irrespective of your nationality.

5 Egyptian Consulates

If you wish to organize your Egyptian visa in advance or have any queries, a complete list of Egyptian embassies and consulates can be found on the following website: *www.embassyworld.com*

6 Egyptian National Tourist Offices

For brochures, maps and upcoming events, contact the Egyptian Tourist Office in your own country. *UK: 170 Piccadilly, London. 020 7493 5283 • USA: 645 North Michigan Avenue, Suite 829, Chicago. 514 861 8071 • Canada: 1253 McGill College Avenue, Suite 250, Montreal, Quebec. 514 861 4420.*

7 Tourist Offices in Egypt

There are tourist offices in all of the large towns and cities in Egypt, but they tend to be of little use with uninformed staff and little in the way of maps or other printed material. Hotel desks are usually a better source of up-to-date information, but the best advice is to get hold of all the maps and guides you think you'll need before leaving home.

8 Time and Electricity

Egypt is two hours ahead of Greenwich Mean Time in winter, which means it is two hours ahead of the UK and seven hours ahead of the US East Coast. Egypt's clocks move forward for Daylight Savings Time, usually on the last Friday in April and back again on the last Thursday in September. Electricity is 220V and sockets are for round-pronged, twin-pin plugs.

9 Insurance

Travellers should take out both health and personal belongings insurance. Although it is possible to get good medical assistance in Egypt, it has to be paid for (state facilities should definitely be avoided) and the best hospitals and doctors are expensive. If you have anything stolen you need to obtain an official theft report, called a *mahdar*, from the police.

10 What to Take

You can buy most things in Egypt but you should bring your own sunscreen. You should also bring any prescription or non-prescription medicines. Egyptian pharmacies are very good, but drugs may go under unrecognizable names.

Preceding pages **Interior view of a coffee house**

  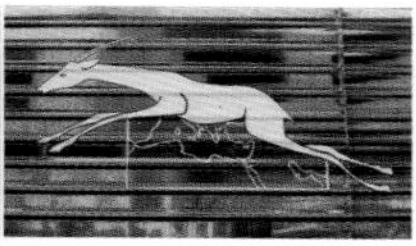

Left **Overnight sleeper train** Centre **Cairo taxi** Right **Superjet long-distance bus logo**

TOP 10 Getting There and Around

1 By Air From Europe

Flying to Egypt from the UK takes five to six hours. There are international airports at Alexandria, Cairo and Luxor, although most major carriers fly into Cairo only. Major airlines flying direct from the UK to Egypt include British Airways, BMI and EgyptAir, although you may get cheaper fares with other carriers that involve a change of flights, such as Air France via Paris, for example.

2 By Intercontinental Air

From the USA, EgyptAir flies direct to Cairo daily. Delta Air Lines operates five flights a week from New York. A number of European and Gulf airlines serve Cairo from a wider range of departure points, but New York still offers by far the biggest choice of airlines.

3 Packages and Charter Flights

The best-value flights are with the growing number of charter packages and low-cost carriers, most of which fly directly to Luxor, rather than Cairo. Just type "Luxor cheap flights" into an Internet search engine to be presented with all-inclusive flight and hotel deals at very low prices.

4 Domestic Flights

Internal flights are operated by EgyptAir. It connects both Luxor and Aswan with Cairo. Flying time in both cases is around one hour and flying Cairo–Luxor costs around £E600 one way.

5 Egypt's Airports

Cairo airport is around 20 km (12 miles) north-east of the city centre. There is no adequate public transport and the only realistic option is to take a taxi, which costs around £E80 to central Cairo. Luxor and Aswan airports are much easier to negotiate and are far closer to their respective city centres.

6 Train

The only real alternative to flying between Cairo and Luxor and Aswan is the train. There are two tourist trains, both of which travel overnight and have sleeper carriages. They depart Cairo around 9pm and arrive in Luxor about 6am the next day. For schedules, prices and bookings, visit https://enr.gov.eg or www.wataniasleepingtrains.com

7 Long-Distance Buses

Buses are the best way to travel between Cairo and destinations such as Alexandria, Port Said and Ismailia. Services are more frequent and faster than trains. Various companies compete on the routes, with Superjet, where available, being the most reputable.

8 Taxis

Within Egypt's towns, by far the most convenient way to get around is by taxi. Taxis are plentiful and, by Western standards, cheap. Avoid black-and-white unmetered taxis. White cabs have working meters and can be hailed on the street. Yellow cabs also have a meter but must be booked by phone. Blue cabs can be more expensive as they charge a flat fee according to distance.
Yellow cabs 16516 • Blue cabs 02 3760 9616

9 Car Hire

Driving in Egypt can be terrifying. Egyptians do not seem to obey any road rules, communicate by means of the horn and are adverse to using headlights at night. If you feel you need the freedom of a car to get around, it isn't any more expensive to hire a car and driver or just negotiate a day rate with a local taxi.

10 Boat

The Nile runs from the very south of Egypt all the way up the middle, exiting into the Mediterranean in the north. Its central stretch, through what is known as Middle Egypt, is open to passenger traffic, and a few specialist cruises make the 10-day journey from Cairo to Luxor or the 14-day trip to Aswan. Overnight trips on feluccas are possible only from Aswan.

Left **Postbox** Centre **National Bank of Egypt** Right **Banknote**

Top 10 Practical Information

1 Business & Shopping Hours

Banks and offices tend to open Sunday to Thursday from 8am or 9am until 5pm. Shops open from around 10am until 9pm or later, but may close for midday prayers on Friday. In Alexandria many shops close from 2pm until 5pm. During Ramadan opening hours become totally unpredictable.

2 Currency

Egypt's basic unit of currency is the Egyptian pound (£E). One pound is divided into 100 piastres (pt). Egyptian banknotes have Arabic numerals on one side, Western numerals on the other and come in denominations from £E5 to £E200. Always carry some smaller notes as the higher value notes can sometimes be difficult to change.

3 Banks & ATMs

Money can be changed at banks and Forex bureaus, which are private moneychangers found in larger towns. Forex bureaus tend to offer better rates than banks but they don't always take traveller's cheques. Automatic Cash Dispensers (ATMs) have proliferated rapidly in recent years, although not all are compatible with international banking cards. The best place to look for ATMs is in the lobby of larger hotels.

4 Credit Cards

Credit cards are accepted in large restaurants and shops and at most hotels, but that's about it. They will not be accepted in smaller shops and in souqs, and you can't buy tickets for sites with them. American Express, MasterCard and Visa are the most likely to be accepted.

5 International Phone Calls

The cheapest way of phoning overseas is to use a telephone office (known as a *centraal*), where you pay at the end of the call. Rates are cheaper 8pm–8am. Most hotels also have an international line.

6 Mobile Phones

Not all networks provide roaming services in Egypt. If you are planning to use your mobile a lot you can buy a SIM card from a local provider such as Mobinil or Vodafone, both of which have shops throughout Egypt. You can then buy top-up cards from kiosks and grocery stores.

7 Internet Access

There are Internet cafés all over Egypt, while many hotels offer an online terminal for guests' use. Charges are around £E10 per hour, although five-star hotels charge considerably more. Wi-Fi is widely available in hotels and cafés.

8 Mail

The best place to buy stamps and post letters is at your hotel. Airmail letters take between around a week to 10 days to the UK and Europe and a couple of weeks to the USA and Australia. If you need to send something quickly, use EMS (Express Mail Service), which is offered by most major post offices. Parcels must be sent via main post offices. In Cairo the main post office is on Midan Ramses.

9 Shipping & Couriers

If you are buying anything sizable, such as an item of furniture or a carpet, then the seller should be able to organize the shipping for you. Private courier firms such as DHL (www.dhl.com) and FedEx (www.fedex.com/eg) do exist in Egypt, with offices in Cairo and Luxor, but they are expensive.

10 Public Conveniences

Public toilets in Egypt are often unsanitary. Take the opportunity to make use of the facilities in hotels, upmarket restaurants and Western-style fast-food franchises and cafés, which tend to be better maintained. Even then there's often no toilet paper so get into the habit of carrying a packet of tissues in your bag.

Left **Sign prohibiting photography** Centre **Typical café** Right **Shoes left outside a mosque**

Top 10 Etiquette

1 Islam

While nowhere near as conservative as Iran or Saudi Arabia, Egypt is an Islamic country. Intimate behaviour in public (such as kissing or even holding hands) will be seen as offensive, and there are considerations of dress to be observed *(see below)*. For more dos and don'ts see p120.

2 Hospitality

Egyptians are genuinely hospitable people, although it's often hard to know when this is the case or the friendly welcome is just an overture that leads to a perfume or papyrus shop. Don't be naïve, but at the same time avoid rudeness or aggressive behaviour in response to insistent offers and demands from would-be guides or salesmen.

3 Dress

Avoid too much exposed skin. Shorts, for both men and women, are not acceptable when walking around town (but are fine on the boat or beach). Women should also avoid skimpy tops that leave shoulders or midriffs bare, and short skirts. However, it is not necessary for women to cover their hair.

4 Female Travellers

Egypt can be a stressful place for solo female travellers to visit. Many women visitors have a problem with persistent sexual harassment, from wolf whistles and lewd comments to furtive gropes or bottom-pinching. Having a male friend along greatly reduces, but unfortunately does not eliminate, the hassle.

5 Photographing People

If you are taking a photograph of somebody, be sure to ask their permission. In rural areas, in particular, Egyptians can be sensitive about having their picture taken and it can sometimes lead to uncomfortable situations if you aren't careful.

6 Other Photographic Considerations

Often Egyptians may stop you taking photographs of things they feel show the country in a "backward" light. Also, photographing bridges, train stations, policemen or police stations – anything that might be considered "strategic" – is absolutely forbidden and may result in your camera being confiscated until you can prove you have deleted the images.

7 Smoking

A large percentage of men in Egypt still smoke and as yet there are few bans on where people can do so. Expect indoor restaurants and cafés to be very smoky.

8 Tipping

A tip *(baksheesh)* is expected by everybody. Anybody that does you any kind of service from carrying bags to looking after your shoes when you visit a mosque will expect a small gratuity. Usually £E2 is sufficient. A temple attendant who opens up a "restricted area" for you will expect something more like £E10.

9 Begging

Egyptians give freely to beggars – it is a requirement of Islam. Children sometimes stand outside supermarkets and ask for food rather than money. What you will encounter as a visitor is lots of children asking for money, which is something quite different, as they prey on tourists. Most Egyptians find them a nuisance too and will shoo them away.

10 Visiting Mosques

Shoes must be removed before entering a mosque and there are often a shoe rack and shoe guardian at the door for this purpose. It is also essential that proper clothing is worn – people wearing shorts or sleeveless T-shirts may be refused admission or offered a shawl to cover up with.

Left **Some places have very little shade** Centre **Holding hands is to be avoided** Right **Mineral water**

Top 10 Things to Avoid

1 Dehydration

It is terrifically hot in Egypt and there is little shade at most tourist sites. Dehydration is a very real threat so drink plenty of fluids (not alcohol or coffee, both of which exacerbate the problem) and put a little extra salt on your food. Bottled water is sold everywhere but it is always wise to carry a bottle with you.

2 Tap Water

Tap water in Egypt is heavily chlorinated and relatively safe to drink but if you are not used to it, it could still upset your stomach. For this reason it is best to stick to sealed bottles of mineral water, which are cheap and readily available throughout the country.

3 Fake Guides

At many historic sites, especially the Pyramids and Karnak, you may be approached by locals offering their services as guides: be wary. Many of these men have next to no knowledge whatsoever and the extent of their commentary runs little further than: "Very big, very old". If you feel you need a guide, consider hiring one in advance through your hotel.

4 Getting Drunk

Alcohol is served in some restaurants, and bars do exist in Egypt, particularly in hotels, but most Egyptians do not drink as they consider it contrary to Islam. Getting drunk is a sure way of demeaning yourself in the eyes of the locals.

5 Drugs

There are drugs around in Egypt. Marijuana is not uncommon in Sinai but there's also a harder drug scene in the cities that is a current cause of consternation. It is all illegal and penalties for anyone found using drugs are harsh. At the very least you will be deported and not allowed to return to the country.

6 Overstretching the Plumbing

Egyptian plumbing is not very robust. Toilets get blocked very easily. For this reason there will often be a wastebasket in the toilet cubicle, which is for used toilet paper. It may not seem particularly hygienic but is preferable to the flooding that will otherwise be the result.

7 Public Displays of Affection

No kissing in public, no holding hands, no walking with arms around each others' waists. Egypt is very conservative and if you want to avoid giving offence this is something couples need to be aware of.

8 Trying to Do Too Much

There is an immense amount to see and do in Egypt, particularly in Cairo and Luxor. Be realistic in your goals. It takes months to see everything, not days. A good plan in Luxor is to sightsee in the mornings, give yourself the afternoon off, and then possibly visit a temple in the evening for the Sound and Light show.

9 Losing Your Temper

"Just for looking, just for looking!"– vendors' cries are incessant ("Cheaper than Asda price!"). Every Egyptian you meet seems to want to sell you something ("My brother has very nice perfume shop!"). They are just trying to make a living and it's not easy. So even at the umpteenth tug of your sleeve, keep your cool and just say a polite "No thanks".

10 Believing All You Are Told

General Montgomery did not ride your camel at the Pyramids. Your felucca captain is not called Michael/Chris/Bruce, just the same as you. That yellow powder you are snapping up as a bargain is not saffron. That papyrus is not "very old" but was probably plucked from a banana plant last week... Enjoy Egypt but beware of being too gullible.

Left **Mind pickpockets in crowded streets** Centre **Tourist police** Right **Detail of pharmacy sign**

TOP 10 Security and Health

1 Vaccinations & Other Precautions

There are no compulsory inoculations for Egypt, although you should always be up to date with polio and tetanus vaccinations. It's also worth being vaccinated against typhoid. Egypt is not in a malarial zone.

2 Food Safety

Just as it is unwise to drink the local tap water *(see p120)*, it is also not recommended to eat salads as the vegetables will have been rinsed under the tap. Avoid raw meats and anything that looks undercooked, and always thoroughly wash (in purified water) any fruits that are eaten unpeeled, such as grapes.

3 Stomach Upsets

No matter what precautions are taken, many visitors to Egypt will come down with diarrhoea. If and when you do, keep your bodily fluids topped up with plenty of bottled water and eat only the blandest of foods such as plain boiled rice and vegetables. You may also want to take rehydration salts. Medicines like Imodium should only be used if you have to travel or if the symptoms don't clear up after a couple of days.

4 Mosquitoes

Mosquitoes can be a nuisance. Five-star hotels are usually air-tight and safe, but in cheaper hotels the pests often come as standard. You can employ mosquito coils, rub-on repellent or a plug-in vaporizer, all of which are sold at pharmacies.

5 Animal Dangers

There are snakes and scorpions in Egypt, particularly in the south of the country, but the danger is minimal as they are mostly nocturnal and avoid people. A greater threat comes from the wild dogs that are occasionally encountered roaming city streets in packs. Do not approach them as they are feral and a bite will necessitate precautionary rabies shots.

6 Pharmacies

Egypt's pharmacies are excellent and are usually staffed with well-trained individuals who mostly speak English and who can dispense a wide range of medicines. If you have any health problems in Egypt the pharmacy should be your first port of call. If the pharmacist doesn't know what's wrong they will recommend a doctor.

7 Doctors

Most hotels and better pharmacies should be able to recommend a good English-speaking doctor. They charge for consultations – expect to pay around £E150.

8 Crime

Crime is minimal in Egypt. However, pick-pockets work in Cairo, particularly around Midan Tahrir and on the buses to the Pyramids. Casual theft is no more or less prevalent than in any other country. Take the same precautions you would anywhere – don't leave valuables lying around in plain sight.

9 Tourist Police

If you have a problem or need to report a crime, go to the Tourist Police, who can be found at tourist sites, airports and stations. They are supposed to be trained to assist foreign visitors and should speak a second language, usually English. They dress like normal police but wear an armband reading "Tourist Police".

10 Terrorism and Security

The Egyptian economy is extremely dependent on tourism and the Mubarak government invested heavily in making sure nothing happened to foreign visitors. Since the terror attacks of the late 1990s the country's tourist attractions have been flooded with armed security. No tourists were harmed during the 2011–12 anti-government protests, but it is wise to check the current situation with the Foreign Office before travel.

Left **Copper- and brassware** Centre **Glasses of tea** Right **A shop in a *souq***

TOP 10 Shopping and Eating Tips

1 Haggling

If you shop in the *souqs*, haggling is unavoidable. Prices are never written down; you have to ask and if you agree the first price the shopkeeper names, you will be paying way over the odds. If you want something, look around and ask the price at several different stalls. Then decide how much you are prepared to pay and make an offer well below it.

2 The Offer of Tea

When haggling, just because you accept a cup of tea from the shopkeeper does not mean that you are under any obligation to buy. If you are not happy with the price you should walk away. Bear in mind that however little you pay, a shopkeeper will never sell anything at a loss.

3 What to Buy

Tourist souvenirs are plentiful *(see pp54–5)*. Copper- and brassware (pots, trays and hanging lamps) are particularly worth buying as Egyptian craftsmanship in metalwork is generally excellent. The best jewellery and carpets are produced by the Bedouin and are found only in boutiques, rather than in the *souqs* where the quality can be poor. Spices are cheap and excellent quality, while the opposite is true of clothing.

4 Antiquities

Do not be fooled into buying any sort of antiquity, pharaonic or otherwise, as 99 per cent of these are fakes. And if it is real, you are not allowed to take it out of the country anyway – export of anything dating before the 20th century is illegal.

5 Where to Shop

The most fun places for shopping are the colourful *souqs* in Cairo (Khan al-Khalili is the best) and the *souq* in Aswan. For more unusual items, Cairo has some great boutiques, particularly in the upmarket neighbourhoods of Zamalek and Doqqi *(see p76)*.

6 Types of Restaurants

Egypt doesn't have a strong tradition of dining out and even a city as big as Cairo has surprisingly few good restaurants outside of the five-star hotels. What there is in abundance, however, is good street food, in the form of *fuul, taamiya, kushari* and *fiteer (see pp58–9)*. Kebabs, served simply with bread and salad, are always tasty, too.

7 Vegetarians

The concept of vegetarianism is incomprehensible to most Egyptians. However, given that meat is viewed as a luxury item, most basic menu items are meat-free, such as *fuul, taamiya, kushari* and some types of *fiteer*. Also, many of the meze served in upmarket restaurants are based around beans, pulses, seeds and vegetables, such as hummus, tahini and tabbouleh.

8 Taxes

Although restaurant prices are comparatively cheap compared to the West, bills are subject to a 12 per cent service charge and a 10 per cent sales tax – in other words you pay almost 25 per cent more than the prices listed on the menu.

9 Tipping

In addition to the service charge *(see above)* it is expected that you tip in restaurants. Egyptians always do, and as rich foreigners your waiter will be mortally offended if you don't. The standard is around 10 per cent.

10 Opening Hours

Streetfood vendors tend to keep long hours, often opening around 7am or 8am for breakfast and staying open until after midnight. Restaurants will open for lunch, close in the afternoon and then reopen in the evening, usually from 7pm until 11pm. Few restaurants outside Cairo stay open until very late.

Left **Guide at a temple** Centre **Cruise ship moored at Luxor** Right **Edfu Temple**

TOP 10 Cruise Tips

1 The Options
Nile cruises booked as a package holiday can be good value. Seven nights on a boat plus flights can be cheaper than flights alone. The downside is that you will be on a big boat with hundreds of other tourists. If you have the budget it's worth paying more for a smaller boat with an agency such as Abercrombie and Kent or Voyages Jules Verne. *www.abercrombiekent.co.uk/egypt* • *www.vjv.co.uk*

2 Itineraries
There are two basic itineraries. The most popular is seven nights from Luxor to Aswan and back again. The other option is to sail one way spending two to three nights on board depending on which direction you sail. The ultimate trip is from Cairo to Aswan, taking 14 days; this trip also includes some sites in Middle Egypt, such as Abydos and Dendara.

3 What Will I See?
A typical cruise sails from Luxor, stopping at Edfu and Kom Ombo before spending two nights at Aswan, where you visit Philae and have the option of an extra excursion to Abu Simbel. The return leg visits Esna and, on docking at Luxor, includes a full-day's sightseeing.

4 What to Wear
In addition to light clothes for sightseeing it's worth bringing something slightly more formal for dinner, although none of the boats require jacket and tie. It can get chilly at night on the river so bring something a bit warmer for a late-night drink on deck.

5 Food
Three meals a day are included on all package cruises, with packed lunches for excursions. Meals are buffet, mixing Egyptian with international dishes – something for everyone. The quality of the fare depends on the boat, but at the higher end it is very good indeed.

6 Evening Entertainment
Most boats have a bar or lounge and will host a *galabiyya* party, where all are encouraged to dress in the traditional Egyptian men's robe (sold onboard). Some boats feature local musicians, while the bigger boats have a disco-party every night.

7 Guides
All boats have their own tour guides to shepherd tourists around the ancient sites and answer questions. The more upmarket boats have trained Egyptologists who also deliver lectures about the sites that will be visited on the following day.

8 Booking
For the best choice of Nile cruises go to a specialist such as Nile Cruises Direct or Discover Egypt. Prices are higher at peak times, which include Christmas, New Year and Easter. When booking, avoid berths on the lower decks, which offer the poorest views. *www.nilecruisesdirect.com* • *www.discoveregypt.co.uk*

9 Dahabiyyas
These replicas of 19th-century sailboats are the Rolls-Royces among Nile cruisers. Prices are high, but advantages include gorgeous period surrounds, visits to less crowded archaeological sites and a small number of fellow travellers. Most boats are privately owned by small companies, such as Nour el-Nil and Dahabiyya. *www.nourelnil.com* • *www.dahabiyya.com*

10 Lake Nasser
The lesser-known alternative to a Nile cruise visits Aswan, Abu Simbel and several temples in between *(see p113)*. Luxor is not included but you can visit it independently. Highlights are the lake's unspoilt desert scenery and relative solitude. Tours are usually four or five days, depending on whether you depart from Aswan or Abu Simbel. The best boats are run by Belle Epoque Travel. *http://eugenie.com.eg*

Left **Hotel doorman** Centre **Kempinksi Nile Hotel** Right **Inside the historic Cairo Marriott**

Top 10 Accommodation Tips

1 Staying in Cairo
The most convenient places to stay are by the Nile in central Cairo, which is close to the Egyptian Museum, Khan al-Khalili and Islamic Cairo. A number of five-star hotels are located in the neighbourhood of the Pyramids but this means all the other sites of Cairo are a long taxi-ride away.

2 Luxor and Aswan
Both Luxor and Aswan are small enough that, in terms of location, it doesn't really matter where you stay. All of the best accommodation clusters around the Nile and you should make sure that your room has river views. An interesting alternative in Luxor is to stay on the relatively undeveloped West Bank, where facilities tend to be more basic but this is compensated for by the timeless rural setting.

3 Price Considerations
Prices are highest around Christmas, New Year and Easter, and also during the Islamic feasts of Eid al-Adha and Eid al-Fitr, which fall at the end of Ramadan. Conversely, out of season (June–August), it is often possible to get some excellent deals. Rates are usually quoted in US dollars, although if paying by cash you do so in Egyptian pounds.

4 Making Reservations
Most Egyptian hotels and hostels have Internet booking, but you should follow up with an email and print out the confirmation. Egyptian hoteliers are famously slipshod when it comes to bookings and it is not unheard of for guests to turn up and find their reservation has not been recorded.

5 Finding Something on the Spot
Tourism has suffered after the 2011 Revolution, and it is now easier to find accommodation without advance booking, especially out of season (June–August). Travelling without a reservation at other times is not recommended. All the best places get booked up in advance, particularly at peak times.

6 Tipping
Service workers are badly paid in Egypt and tipping the staff is never amiss. Leave something in your room for the maids, and give porters who carry your bags to your room £E5.

7 Hidden Extras
Hotel rooms are subject to about an extra 20 per cent in taxes. Two- or three-star hotels may charge extra for fridge, air conditioning and TV. Check when booking that the rate quoted is all-inclusive.

8 Historic Hotels
You can book yourself into a piece of history at a number of historic hotels *(see pp52–3)* mostly built in the late 19th century when Egypt was enjoying its first tourist boom. Many of these properties are now managed by international hotel chains and offer all the facilities expected of a five-star establishment, but with added period charm.

9 Hotel Touts
Tourists arriving at the railway station in Luxor or Aswan are swamped by touts offering cheap rooms. Most are hustling for commissions. The hotel they recommend is simply the one that charges the highest commission – and most often it's the seediest hotels that need the help of the touts to fill their rooms. The tout's commission will be added to your bill.

10 Hotel Rerouting
In Cairo some taxi drivers ferrying tourists from the airport top up their earnings by touting for hotels. They may tell you that the hotel for which you're heading is now closed and they can recommend somewhere better. This is not true and the recommended hotel is paying drivers for any guests they can steer its way.

Price Categories

For a standard, double room per night (with breakfast if included), taxes and extra charges.	£	under £E350
	££	£E350–700
	£££	£E700–1,000
	££££	£E1,000–1,500
	£££££	over £E1,500

Mena House Oberoi

Top 10 Top-End Hotels in Cairo

1 Cairo Marriott

The former palace has undergone a great deal of change but it still boasts some glorious public spaces and the nicest garden in town *(see p52)*. *Map E2 • 16 Sharia Saraya al-Gezira, Zamalek • 02 2728 3000 • www.marriott.com • £££*

2 Villa Belle Epoque

This 1920s villa with 13 period-style rooms, beautiful leafy gardens, pool and conservatory dining room is Cairo's first boutique hotel. It is in the leafy Ma'adi suburb, 10 km (6 miles) south of central Cairo. *Map J2 • Short walk from Rd 9, Maadi • 02 2516 9656 • www.villabelleepoque.com • £££££*

3 Conrad International

The Conrad is one of the city's most luxurious hotels – it has five executive levels, a health club, a casino and a helipad. The restaurants are superb. Next door is an upmarket shopping mall, but otherwise you need a taxi to get anywhere. *Map E1 • 1191 Corniche al-Nil, Bulaq • 02 2580 8000 • www.conradhotels3.hilton.com • ££££*

4 Four Seasons Nile Plaza

There are two Four Seasons hotels in town (the other is the Four Seasons at the First Residence). Both are superb, but this is the newer of the two and has a more central location. *Map E5 • 1089 Corniche al-Nil, Garden City • 02 2791 7000 • www.fourseasons.com/caironp • £££££*

5 Grand Nile Tower

A vast, 715-room hotel, the Nile Tower sits commandingly on the very northern tip of the island of Rhoda, just south of central Cairo. Most rooms enjoy fantastic Nile views and the facilities are first class. *Map E5 • Corniche al-Nil, Rhoda • 02 2365 1234 • www.grandniletower.com • £££££*

6 Mena House Oberoi

The hotel with the most distinguished pedigree of any in Egypt opened in 1869 and has played host to generations of world leaders and royals. The location beside the Pyramids is unique, but make sure to book rooms in the main building and not in the modern garden annex *(see p52)*. *Map H2 • Pyramids Road, Giza • 02 3377 3222 • www.oberoimenahouse.com • ££££*

7 Fairmont Nile City

Located within the Nile City Towers complex, this hotel boasts a great spa and a rooftop pool and trendy bar. Blending state-of-the-art technology with Art Deco design, many of its 566 rooms enjoy panoramic views of the river and the distant pyramids. *Map E1 • Nile City Towers, 2005B Corniche al-Nil, Ramlet Bulaq • 02 2461 9494 • www.fairmont.com/nile-city-cairo • £££££*

8 Kempinski Nile Hotel

Guests here can enjoy butler service, a luxury spa and a rooftop pool with stunning views. Its Osmanly restaurant *(see p60)* serves exceptional Turkish food. *Map E5 • Corniche al-Nil, 12 Sharia Ahmed Ragheb, Garden City • 02 2798 0000 • www.kempinski.com • £££££*

9 Semiramis InterContinental

This is possibly the best-located hotel in town – it is on the river, just south of Midan Tahrir. River-facing rooms have fine views of the Opera House on the island of Gezira. There are a couple of excellent hotel restaurants and good facilities all round. *Map E4 • Corniche al-Nil, Garden City • 02 2795 7171 • www.ichotelsgroup.com • £££*

10 Sofitel al-Gezira

This is one of Cairo's most stylish hotels. Public spaces look stunning and as the hotel is a cylindrical tower on the southern tip of the island of Gezira, all rooms have terrific Nile views. *Map D–E5 • 3 Sharia al-Majlis al-Thawra, Gezira • 02 2737 3737 • www.sofitel.com • £££*

Unless otherwise stated, all rooms have en-suite bathrooms and air conditioning

Left **Flamenco** Centre **Talisman Hotel de Charme** Right **Cosmopolitan Hotel**

Top 10 Mid-Range Hotels in Cairo

1 Flamenco
The Flamenco is a well-maintained business hotel in a fashionable area full of cafés and restaurants. It has two bars and a good Spanish restaurant. It's worth paying the premium for a room with a view of the Nile. *Map D1 • 2 Sharia al-Gezira al-Wusta, Zamalek • 02 2735 0815 • www.flamencohotels.com/cairo/home.php • ££*

2 Hotel President
It is often possible to get bargain rates through on-line booking agencies at this three-star hotel. Although located some distance from the main sights, the backstreets of Zamalek are lively with plenty of good cafés, bars and restaurants. *Map D1 • 22 Taha Hussein, Zamalek • 02 2735 0718 • www.presidenthotelcairo.com • ££*

3 Havana Hotel
A small Anglo-Egyptian, family-run hotel, the Havana is well looked after and the staff are very welcoming. Mohandiseen is a 10-minute taxi ride from Downtown. *Map H1 • 26 Sharia Syria, Mohandiseen • 02 3749 0758 • www.havanahotelcairo.com • ££*

4 Talisman Hotel de Charme
Quite close to being a boutique hotel in terms of style and service, the Talisman's rooms are decorated in rich colours, while common areas are filled with examples of Egyptian arts and crafts. It's a stunning hotel in a great location. *Map G3 • 39 Sharia Talaat Harb, Downtown • 02 2393 9431 • ££*

5 Oasis Hotel
If you are considering staying by the Pyramids the Oasis offers good value for money: spacious, comfortable rooms; free shuttle bus Downtown; numerous restaurants and bars; and an attractive garden swimming pool. *Map H2 • Cairo–Alexandria Desert Road • 02 3838 7333 • www.oasis.com.eg • £££*

6 Cosmopolitan Hotel
This historic, lovely Art Nouveau-era hotel doesn't quite live up to the old-world grandeur of its foyer. Rooms are very basic, but the location is excellent and the room rates are usually highly competitive *(see p52)*. *Map F3 • 1 Sharia Ibn Talab, off Sharia Qasr al-Nil, Downtown • 02 2392 3956 • ££*

7 Pyramisa Suites Hotel
The Ministry of Tourism classes this as a five-star hotel; it is not, but then neither are its mid-range prices, for which you get large rooms in a modern establishment a short taxi ride from central Cairo. Make sure to ask for an inward-facing pool-view room, and not one on the main road. *Map D5 • 60 Sharia al-Giza, Doqqi • 02 3336 7000 • www.pyramisaegypt.com • £££*

8 Grand Hotel
Built in 1939, the Grand is situated in the bustling heart of Downtown. The rooms are clean and its marbled bathrooms are divine, but most period fixtures have gone. Dinner is available, but no alcohol is served. *Map G3 • 17 Sharia 26th July, Downtown • 02 2575 7700 • www.grandhotelcairo.com • ££*

9 Carlton Hotel
This central hotel dating back to 1935 retains many of its original features. Rooms are large, if a little unstylish, and amenities include free Wi-Fi and a rooftop bar-restaurant. One meal a day is included in the rate. *Map F3 • 21 Sharia 26th July, Downtown • 012 2776 1192 • www.carltonhotelcairo.com • £*

10 Hotel Longchamps
With only 21 rooms, the Longchamps tends to be booked weeks in advance. It's an atmospheric hotel with clean, homely rooms and a fine restaurant, and there are plenty of shops and restaurants nearby. *Map D1 • 21 Sharia Ismail Mohammed, Zamalek • 02 2735 2311 • www.hotellongchamps.com • ££*

Unless otherwise stated, all rooms have en-suite bathrooms and air conditioning

Price Categories

For a standard, double room per night (with breakfast if included), taxes and extra charges.

£	under £E350
££	£E350–700
£££	£E700–1,000
££££	£E1,000–1,500
£££££	over £E1,500

Above **Hotel Longchamps**

Top 10 Budget Hotels in Cairo

1 Victoria Hotel

The Victoria is about a century old and is located approximately a 10-minute walk from the Egyptian Museum. It's cleaner and better looked after than many hotels in this price range and has a small garden and appealing period bar. *Map G2 • 66 Sharia al-Gumhuriyya, Downtown • 02 2589 2290 • www.victoriahotel-egypt.com • ££*

2 Windsor Hotel

Almost nothing has been changed since the 1950s at Cairo's most authentic period hotel – not so great perhaps when it comes to its plumbing and spartan furnishings, but this hotel is loved for its colonial air *(see p52). Map G3 • 19 Sharia Alfy Bey, Downtown • 02 2591 5810 • www.windsorcairo.com • ££*

3 Mayfair

This quiet hotel in an attractive 1930s residential block has a nice breakfast terrace, free Wi-Fi and a kitchen. Not all rooms have air conditioning. *Map D2 • 9 Sharia Aziz Osman, Zamalek • 02 2735 7315 • www.mayfaircairo.com • £*

4 Al-Hussein

This is one of the few hotels in the heart of medieval Cairo. Rooms are very basic, although they include a fridge and some have air conditioning. It is noisy but there's so much going on outside your balcony that you may not want to sleep anyway. *Map J3 • Midan al-Hussein, entered from the passage that leads to Fishawi's coffee house • 02 2591 8089 • £*

5 Garden City House Hotel

A little run-down (although clean), this remains one of Cairo's best budget options thanks to its friendly and helpful staff. The location is also excellent, just two minutes' walk from Midan Tahrir. *Map F4 • 23 Sharia Kamal al-Din Salah, Downtown • 02 2794 8400 • www.gardencityhouse.com • £*

6 Pension Roma

Usually booked solid, the Roma has a pleasant old-world elegance. Rooms vary – some are enormous and several have air conditioning. *Map G3 • 169 Sharia Mohammed Farid, Downtown • 02 2391 1088 • www.pensionroma.com.eg • £*

7 Odeon Palace Hotel

While there is nothing palatial about the Odeon, its rooms are large, although a little worn around the edges. The 24-hour rooftop bar is popular with expats. *Map F3 • 6 Sharia Abdel Hamid Said, Downtown • 02 2577 6637 • www.hodeon.com • ££*

8 Horus House Hotel

More like a European B&B than a hotel, this is a small, friendly family-run establishment on a quiet residential street. Rooms vary in quality – ask for one that has been recently renovated. There's a nice terrace, a breakfast room and a small 24-hour bar. *Map D1 • 21 Sharia Ismail Mohammed, Zamalek • 02 2735 3634 • www.horushousehotel.4t.com • £*

9 Hotel Osiris

The Osiris is a modern, cosy hotel decorated in a unique Oriental-inspired style. Located in the heart of Downtown, it offers quiet rooms, comfortable beds, an Internet café and a rooftop terrace with a panoramic view of Cairo, as well as a restaurant serving delicious home-made Egyptian food. *Map F4 • 49 Sharia Nubar, Bab al-Louq, Downtown • 02 2794 5728 • www.hotelosiris.fr • ££*

10 Lotus Hotel

A hotel for the truly budget-conscious, the Lotus dates from 1950, as is still reflected by the mattresses. However, the location, just off Midan Tahrir, is superb. The staff are friendly and it's a great place to meet fellow travellers. *Map F4 • 12 Sharia Talaat Harb • 02 2575 0966 • www.lotushotel.com • £*

Left **Windsor Palace, Alexandria** Centre **Mercure Forsan Island** Right **Cecil Hotel, Alexandria**

Top 10 Hotels Beyond Cairo

1 Four Seasons Hotel Alexandria

A luxurious hotel, the Four Seasons has its own beach and marina, a spa and a circular infinity pool on a fourth-floor terrace. All rooms have sea views. *Map S2 • 399 Sharia al-Geish, San Stefano • 03 581 8000 • www.fourseasons.com/alexandria • £££££*

2 Al-Salamlek, Alexandria

Al-Salamlek more than makes up for a fairly remote, if picturesque, location in former royal gardens, 11 km (7 miles) east of Alexandria city centre. Once a lodge for royal guests, it recreates a *belle époque* experience *(see p53). Map T1 • Montazah • 03 547 7999 • www.elsalamlekpalace.com • £££££*

3 Cecil Hotel, Alexandria

Alexandria's most famous hotel gained its fame in the 1930s–40s when it was one of the city's glitziest social venues. It is now in its dotage but still boasts a superb central location and period charm *(see p53). Map S2 • 16 Midan Saad Zaghloul • 03 487 7173 • www.sofitel.com • ££££*

4 Metropole, Alexandria

The Metropole is one of Alexandria's grand old hotels. Clumsy makeovers have obscured some of the period detail, but the rooms are large and many have views over the central square and the attractive Eastern Harbour *(see p53). Map S2 • 52 Sharia Saad Zaghloul • 03 486 1467 • www.paradiseinnegypt.com • £££*

5 Windsor Palace, Alexandria

Perched since 1906 on the Corniche facing the sea, the Palace is an old hotel with "cage lifts" and high-ceilinged rooms. Facilities are limited but if you get a sea-facing room you'll spend all your time soaking up the view. *Map S2 • Corniche, Eastern Harbour • 03 480 8700 • www.paradiseinnegypt.com • £££*

6 Union Hotel, Alexandria

The best of Alexandria's budget options, the Union is on the Corniche facing the sea, although not many rooms actually enjoy the view. Some rooms can also be tiny and not all have en-suite bathrooms, so consider paying a little extra for a deluxe room on the upper floor. *Map S2 • Corniche, Eastern Harbour • 03 480 7312 • £*

7 Crillon Hotel, Alexandria

After the Union the Crillon is Alexandria's next best budget hotel. Within an old apartment block, rooms vary in size and facilities, and not all have en-suite bathrooms, but the best provide great value. *Map S2 • 5 Sharia Adeeb Ishtak, off the Corniche, Eastern Harbour • 03 480 0330 • £*

8 Hotel de la Poste, Port Said

Entering the Hotel de la Poste is like stepping back in time. Although renovated, it retains many of its early 20th-century fixtures. The high-ceilinged rooms are basic but have fans. Except for a small restaurant and bar, facilities are sparse, but the location is central. *Map B1 • Sharia al-Gumhurriya • 066 322 4048 • £*

9 Resta Port Said

At the north end of town by the mouth of the Suez Canal, this is a modern, international hotel with sea views. Rooms are well equipped and there are restaurants, a small shopping centre and a pool. *Map B1 • Sharia Sultan Hussein • 066 332 5511 • www.restahotels.com • ££££*

10 Mercure Forsan Island, Ismailia

The Mercure is a modern hotel in a fabulous setting of large leafy grounds on the edge of the Suez Canal. It has a private beach where you can sunbathe and watch the tankers sail by. *Map B2 • Forsan Island • 064 391 6316 • www.mercure.com • ££–£££*

Unless otherwise stated, all rooms have en-suite bathrooms and air conditioning

Opulent interior of Al-Moudira

Price Categories

For a standard, double room per night (with breakfast if included), taxes and extra charges.	£	under £E350
	££	£E350–700
	£££	£E700–1,000
	££££	£E1,000–1,500
	£££££	over £E1,500

Top 10 Luxury Hotels in Luxor

1 Winter Palace
The oldest hotel in town is still the finest. Rooms have high ceilings and bathrooms the size of tennis courts. The views from the front rooms across the Nile to the West Bank are unbeatable *(see p53)*. *Map Y2–3 • Corniche al-Nil, East Bank • 095 2380 425 • www.sofitel.com • ££–££££*

2 Sofitel Karnak
About 6 km (4 miles) from Luxor town centre, this is a stylish hotel set within its own extensive gardens filled with palm trees and bougainvillea. There are tennis courts and a swimming pool by the Nile. *Map Z4 • El Zinia Gebly Street, East Bank • 095 237 8020 • www.sofitel.com • ££*

3 Sheraton Luxor Resort
At the very southern end of Luxor town, the Sheraton is nevertheless a short walk from the main shop and restaurant strip. The garden setting beside the Nile is attractive, but be warned – only the upper floors have Nile views. *Map X6 • Sharia Khaled Ibn al-Walid, Awamiya, East Bank • 095 227 4544 • www.starwoodhotels.com • ££–£££*

4 Pyramisa Isis
The Pyramisa is a five-star complex within a large garden by the Nile. Rooms are good value and, in the strangely named Pink Panda, it has Upper Egypt's only Chinese restaurant. *Map X6 • Sharia Khaled Ibn al-Walid, East Bank • 095 237 0100 • www.pyramisaegypt.com • ££*

5 Al-Moudira
In a remote location and surrounded by sugar-cane fields, Al-Moudira is an oasis – a low-rise hotel of traditional mud-brick architecture set in lush gardens. Rooms are spacious and striking. A real experience. *Map B4 • Haggar Daba'iyya, 5 km (3 miles) from Luxor Bridge, West Bank • 012 325 1307 • www.moudira.com • £££££*

6 Hilton Luxor Resort & Spa
Just north of the temple of Karnak, this is Luxor's most luxurious hotel. Facilities include the Nayara Spa with two elevated infinity pools overlooking the Nile and seven restaurants and bars. If money is no object, this is your option. *Map Z2 • New Karnak, Luxor • 095 237 4933 • www3.hilton.com • £££££*

7 Maritim Jolie Ville Kings Island
Accommodation is in bungalows among palm trees on the hotel's own island just south of Luxor (there is a free shuttle). This is a relaxing resort, great for walking and birdwatching. *Map B4 • Kings Island • 095 227 4855 • www.jolieville-hotels.com • ££–££££*

8 El-Luxor Hotel
Midway between Luxor Temple and the Luxor Museum, the El-Luxor boasts a good location and has an appealing pool. Aim to get a room with a Nile view and set your alarm for 6am to watch the hot-air balloons drifting above the West Bank. *Map Z1 • Corniche al-Nil, East Bank • 095 238 0944 • www.el-luxor-hotel.com • ££–£££*

9 Steigenberger Nile Palace Luxor
Rooms are comfortable, large and well equipped in this highly rated hotel by the Nile. The house restaurants (including Lebanese, Thai and Italian) are good and service is excellent. *Map X6 • Sharia Khaled Ibn al-Walid • 095 236 6999 • www.steigenberger.com/luxor • ££–£££*

10 Sonesta St George
One of the swankiest hotels on the strip south of town, the Sonesta has full amenities, including pool and sunbeds. Service and staff are excellent. There is a pontoon area beside the Nile, which is wonderful for watching the sun set over the West Bank. *Map X6 • Corniche al-Nil, East Bank • 095 238 2575 • www.sonesta.com/Luxor • £££*

Due to a decline in tourist numbers, many luxury hotels are offering large discounts

Left **Hotel Sheherazade** Centre **Marsam Hotel** Right **El-Gezira Hotel**

Top 10 Good-Value Hotels in Luxor

1 Gaddis Hotel

The Gaddis offers faded three-star amenities, but often at very competitive rates. It has pleasant rooms, free Wi-Fi, a pool and is conveniently located close to many restaurants. *Map X6 • Sharia Khaled Ibn al-Walid, East Bank • 095 238 2838 • www.gaddis-luxor.co.uk • £*

2 Windsor Hotel

Located one block away from the Corniche near the Luxor Museum, the Windsor is slightly shabby but the staff are friendly. It has a small courtyard swimming pool and most rooms have a balcony. *Map Z1 • Sharia Nefertiti, East Bank • 095 237 5547 • £*

3 Al-Nakhil

Situated on the edge of the small village of Al-Gezira a few minutes' walk from the ferry landing on the West Bank, Al-Nakhil provides a chance to sample local life. While a small hotel, the staff are friendly and it is beautifully decorated and surrounded by palm trees. *Map X5 • Bairat al-Gezira, West Bank • 095 2313 922 • www.el-nakhil.com • £*

4 Nefertiti Hotel

In as central a location as is possible, this hotel overlooks Luxor Temple. Although a budget hotel, it is classy, friendly and well looked after. It also has a good café and restaurant. *Map Y2 • Off Sharia Karnak, East Bank • 095 237 2386 • www.nefertitihotel.com • £*

5 Saint Joseph Hotel

From the outside this hotel is less than inspiring; rooms are also rather dated, but they are spacious and they have balconies – make sure to book one that faces the Nile. There is also a rooftop restaurant-bar and a small pool. *Map X6 • Sharia Khalid Ibn al-Walid, East Bank • 095 238 1707 • £*

6 Hotel Sheherazade

The architecture of the Sheherazade is stunning and reflects the traditional Islamic style described in the book *One Thousand and One Arabian Nights*. The rooms are homely and comfortable. This is an exceptional hotel in Al-Gezira village, just by the ferry landing. *Map X5 • Bairat al-Gezira, West Bank • 0100 6115 939 • www.hotelsheherazade.com • £*

7 Philippe Hotel

Situated near the Luxor Museum, just off the Corniche, this three-star hotel has 69 rooms that are pleasant, if a little impersonal and old-fashioned. It has a roof garden with a swimming pool from which there are good views over the Nile. *Map Z1 • Sharia Dr Labib Habachi, East Bank • 095 237 2284 • www.philippeluxorhotel.com • £*

8 New Pola Hotel

A budget option among the five-star hotels on Luxor's main hotel strip, this is a modern, high-rise hotel with good views from upper Nile-facing rooms. It has shaded gardens and a rooftop pool. *Map X6 • Sharia Khalid Ibn al-Walid, East Bank • 095 236 5081 • www.newpolahotel.com • £*

9 El-Gezira Hotel & Gezira Gardens

The Al-Gezira is a popular budget hotel with a roof garden, a minute's walk from the West Bank ferry landing. Nearby, the Gezira Gardens is a mini-holiday village of self-catering apartments sleeping four right by the Nile. *Map X5 • Bairat al-Gezira, West Bank • 095 231 0034 • www.el-gezira.com • £*

10 Marsam Hotel

Located among the ancient monuments, the Marsam was built for American archaeologists in the 1920s. It has 30 simple mudbrick rooms, some with private baths and air conditioning, set around a courtyard and a lovely garden. *Map V3 • Gurna, West Bank • 0100 342 6471 • £*

Unless otherwise stated, all rooms have en-suite bathrooms and air conditioning

Price Categories		
For a standard, double room per night (with breakfast if included), taxes and extra charges.	£	under £E350
	££	£E350–700
	£££	£E700–1,000
	££££	£E1,000–1,500
	£££££	over £E1,500

Above **Isis Island Hotel, Aswan**

Top 10 Top Aswan & Abu Simbel Hotels

1 Old Cataract, Aswan
This is Aswan's grand old hotel, built in 1899 on the finest site in all Egypt overlooking the first cataract of the Nile. Part of Sofitel's range of hotels, the interior is executed in a beautiful neo-Islamic style *(see p53)*. *Map S6 • Sharia Abtal al-Tahrir • 097 231 6000 • www.sofitel.com • £££££*

2 Mövenpick Resort Aswan
This hotel is reached by boat. It enjoys a terrific setting amidst the palm groves on the northern tip of Elephantine Island and has good facilities, spectacular views and a lovely swimming pool. *Elephantine Island • Map S5 • 097 230 34 55 • www.moevenpick-hotels.com • ££££–£££££*

3 Isis Island Hotel, Aswan
A large five-star hotel that occupies its own island just to the south of Aswan, the Isis has a full array of facilities, including two swimming pools and a spa. Guests are ferried to the shore by private launch. *Map R6 • Isis Island • 097 231 7400 • www.pyramisaegypt.com • £££*

4 Basma Hotel, Aswan
Perched on Aswan's highest hill, the Basma offers a panoramic view over the Nile. Its richly-planted gardens harbour a large, heated and floodlit swimming pool. The 189 rooms may be a little dated but are a generous size. *Map S6 • Sharia Al-Fanadek • 097 231 0901 • www.basmahotel.com • ££–£££*

5 AnaKato Nubian House, Aswan
On the edge of a friendly village on the West Bank, AnaKato ("Our House") consists of three colourful Nubian-style buildings featuring 19 large rooms. Guests can enjoy the scenery from private balconies or the quaint patio. Rates include half-board, as well as free pick-up and drop-off by motorboat. *Gharb Soheil, El Noba • 0100 0006 600 • www.anakato.com • £££*

6 Isis Corniche Hotel, Aswan
On the Corniche in the centre of Aswan, this is a small resort hotel, not as fancy as some of the competition but with decent rooms and a swimming pool beside the river. The hotel faces the northern end of Elephantine Island. *Map T5 • Corniche al-Nil • 097 231 5200 • ££*

7 Marhaba Hotel, Aswan
This large modern hotel near the train station has rooms of a decent size but some bathrooms are poorly maintained. Make sure to get a balcony facing the Nile as views are excellent. Room prices are open to negotiation. *Map T4 • Corniche al-Nil • 097 233 0102 • www.marhaba-aswan.com • ££*

8 Philae Hotel, Aswan
The location of the Philae can't be faulted: on the Corniche facing the Nile, with the Aswan *souq* one block behind it and the ferry to Elephantine Island almost opposite. The hotel is modern, with all basic facilities. *Map S5 • 79 Corniche al-Nil • 097 231 2090 • www.philae-hotel.com • ££*

9 Seti Abu Simbel
An overnight stay in Abu Simbel provides the opportunity to see the Temple of Ramses II after the crowds have returned to Aswan. Situated right by Lake Nasser, this is the top hotel in town, with a garden and three swimming pools that overlook the lake. *Map B6 • Abu Simbel Lake Resort • 097 340 0720 • www.setifirst.com • ££££*

10 Nefertari, Abu Simbel
Although this is not as attractive as the Seti, it is cheaper. Rooms are basic but it is close to the temples and has lake views and a pool. *Map B6 • Abu Simbel • 097 340 0508 • www.nefertarihotelabusimble.net • ££*

Keylany, Aswan

Price Categories

For a standard, double room per night (with breakfast if included), taxes and extra charges.		
	£	under £E350
	££	£E350–700
	£££	£E700–1,000
	££££	£E1,000–1,500
	£££££	over £E1,500

Top 10 Budget Aswan & Abu Simbel Hotels

1 Keylany, Aswan

This simple, small hotel is nevertheless smart and has a lovely rooftop breakfasting area, free Wi-Fi and an Internet café. It has a good location, just off the main *souq* street. *Map T5 • Sharia Kaylany, off Sharia Salah ad-Din • 097 232 3134 • www.keylanyhotel.com • £*

2 Nuba Nile Hotel, Aswan

Located just off the square in front of the railway station, this hotel is a decent budget option, with friendly staff. Although rooms are rather tired, they have a fridge and satellite television. *Map T4 • Sharia Abtal al-Tahrir, off Midan al-Mahatta • 097 231 3553 • £*

3 El Salam Hotel, Aswan

With friendly staff, this hotel offers rooms that, despite being somewhat faded, are clean, with fresh sheets and towels, and reliable hot water and air conditioning. Some have large balconies overlooking the Nile. Wi-Fi and a simple breakfast are included in the price. *Map S5 • 101 Corniche al-Nil • 097 230 2651 • £*

4 Orchida St George, Aswan

Centrally located on a pedestrianized street near the Corniche, this hotel has a small rooftop swimming pool with great views of the Nile. There is also a large restaurant. *Map T5 • Sharia Mohammed Khalid, Corniche al-Nil • 097 231 5997 • www.orchida-sg-hotel.com • £*

5 Sara Hotel, Aswan

If you are in Aswan to get away from it all, this may be the hotel to choose – it's built on a clifftop overlooking the Nile about two miles south of town. It boasts fantastic views over the first cataract and the desert beyond. Rooms are spotless and there's a good-sized swimming pool. A shuttle bus runs into town hourly. *Map C5 • Sharia al-Fanadek, Medinat Nasr • 097 232 7234 • www.sarahotel-aswan.com • £*

6 Nile Hotel, Aswan

Centrally located on the Corniche near the local ferry across to Elephantine Island, this is a modern hotel offering 30 rooms, all with wonderful Nile views. It has a restaurant, rooftop bar and Wi-Fi. *Map S5 • 15 Corniche al-Nil • 097 231 4222 • www.nilehotel-aswan.com • £*

7 Noorhan, Aswan

A major backpacker haunt, just a few minutes' walk south of the railway station, the accommodation at the Noorhan is very basic but rooms do have either air conditioning or fans. This is the place to meet other independent travellers. *Map T4 • Off Sharia Souq • 097 231 6069 • £*

8 Nubian Oasis Hotel, Aswan

This is a perennial backpacker favourite, although more for the atmosphere and camaraderie rather than the quality of the facilities. The rooms with bathrooms cost extra. It has a lounge and roof garden where beer is served. *Map T4 • 234 Sharia Saad Zaghloul • 097 231 2126 • £*

9 Bet el Kerem, Aswan

Owned by a Dutch/Nubian couple this is an apartment house by the Nile within walking distance of the ferry. It has nine double rooms and is ideal for groups and families. *Map S4 • Nagh al-Kuba, West Bank • 012 2391 1052 • www.betelkerem.com • £*

10 Eskaleh EcoLodge, Abu Simbel

Run by a Nubian musician and his family this is a charming lodge built in traditional style with five rooms and an excellent restaurant. It doubles as a Nubian cultural centre. *Map B6 • 3 km (2 miles) south of Abu Simbel • 012 368 0521 • £*

Unless otherwise stated, all rooms have en-suite bathrooms and air conditioning

Left **A dahabiyya operated by Nour El Nil** Right **Philae**

Top 10 Cruise Ships

1 Philae
It is designed to look like a Mississippi paddle steamer, but no luxury is spared on this boat managed by Oberoi Hotels. The refurbished cabins and suites all have their own balconies and are catered to by a butler service. *www.oberoihotels.com*

2 Radamis I & II
These two large boats are operated by the Mövenpick group. Slightly cheaper than the smaller cruise ships, their facilities are nevertheless five-star, and there are options of four-day, five-day and eight-day packages. *www.movenpick-nilecruises.com*

3 Sudan
One of the most exclusive vessels on the Nile, the Sudan was built in the late 19th century and used by King Fouad I of Egypt and Sudan, and during the filming of the film version of Agatha Christie's *Death on the Nile*. Each cabin has its own small balcony. *www.steam-ship-sudan.com*

4 Sun Boat III & IV
These are two beautiful vessels operated by Abercrombie & Kent, one of the leading tour agencies specializing in Egypt. Boat III takes just 36 passengers, while Boat IV carries 80 passengers. Facilities and service on both boats are top-class and include an onboard Egyptologist. *www.abercrombiekent.co.uk/egypt*

5 SS Misr & SS Karim
The steamer *SS Misr* was built in 1918 and was used by King Farouk *(see p65)*, while the smaller *SS Karim* is even older and was also formerly used by royalty. Both boats are charming, especially the *SS Karim*, which has the ambience of a floating gentleman's club. The boats are leased to the high-end travel company Voyage Jules Verne. *www.vjv.com*

6 Star Goddess
The Sonesta Collection of Hotels, Resorts and Cruises operates five Nile cruisers, including the standard *Moon Goddess* and *Sun Goddess*. The *Star Goddess* is the most exclusive ship and has 33 suites named after composers, each with its own terrace and full-size bathtub. *www.sonesta.com/NileCruises*

7 Assouan, Al-Nil, Meroe & Malouka
All four of these boats, operated by Nour El Nil, are dahabiyyas – replicas of the old-style sailboats that ferried 19th-century passengers up the Nile. They all carry only 16–20 passengers in languorous luxury, taking six days to sail from Luxor to Aswan. *www.nourelnil.com*

8 MS Semiramis
Thomas Cook & Sons were the first people to start Nile cruising as a commercial concern in the 1870s. The modern-day incarnation of the company offers competitively-priced packages. The *MS Semiramis* is one of the most comfortable of the cruise ships with 66 cabins and full facilities. *www.thomascook.com*

9 SS Kasr Ibrim & Eugénie
The alternative to a Nile cruise is a Lake Nasser cruise. These were the first two boats on the lake and remain the best. Both are grand, *belle époque*-style ships with spacious cabins and luxurious amenities, such as a steam bath on the *Eugénie*. *www.eugenie.com.eg, www.kasribrim.com.eg*

10 MS Tania
One of the less expensive cruise ships that sails Lake Nasser between Aswan and Abu Simbel is this elegant vessel with 28 cabins, which is operated by local Egyptian travel company Travco. *www.travcotels.com*

General Index

Page numbers in **bold** type refer to main entries.

Acknowledgments

The Author
Andrew Humphreys is a travel writer and journalist who spent several years living in Cairo. He has written extensively on Egypt for a variety of publishing companies and was a key contributor to *Eyewitness Egypt*.

Main Photographer
Eddie Gerald

Additional Photography
Max Alexander, Alistair Duncan, Neil Lukas, Ian O'Leary, Rough Guides/Angus Osborn 35br, Rough Guides/Eddie Gerald, Jon Spaull, Peter Wilson.

Maps
Encompass Graphics Ltd

Fact Checker
Anne Tiernan

Indexer
Helen Peters

Proofreader
Huw Hennessy

AT DORLING KINDERSLEY

Publisher
Douglas Amrine

List Manager
Christine Stroyan

Designer and Illustrator
Maite Lantaron

Editor Rada Radojicic

Senior Editor Sadie Smith

Design Manager Sunita Gahir

Designer
Nicola Erdpresser

Picture Researcher
Ellen Root

Cartographic Editor
Stuart James

DTP Designer
Jason Little

Production Controller
Danielle Smith

Revisions Team
Vanessa Betts, Emer FitzGerald, Fay Franklin, Camilla Gersh, Maite Lantaron, Hayley Maher, Catherine Palmi, Sands Publishing Solutions, Conrad van Dyk.

Picture Credits
a = above; b = below/bottom; c = centre; l = left; r =right; t = top.

The publishers would like to thank the following individuals, companies, and picture libraries for permission to reproduce their photographs:

4CORNERS IMAGES: Reinhard Schmid 32-3.

THE ART ARCHIVE: Bibliothèque des Arts Décoratifs Paris/Gianni Dagli Orti 40t; Egyptian Museum Cairo/Gianni Dagli Orti 9bl; Gianni Dagli Orti 29tl.

CORBIS: O. Alamany & E. Vicens 102tr; The Art Archive/ Alfredo Dagli Orti 10tr; Bettmann 42t, 43tl, 49r; Stefano Bianchetti 42br; Gianni Dagli Orti 1, 9tl, 24c, 34bl, 34tc; epa/Khaled

El-Fiqi 62b; epa/Mike Nelson 62tl, 63tl; Free Agents Limited 24crb; Wolfgang Kaehler 31bl; Reed Kaestner 10tc; Araldo de Luca 42c; Jose Fuste Raga 7cr; Sandro Vannini 6cra, 11br, 34c, 34tl; Werner Forman 34tr; Roger Wood 9cra, 10bc, 10tl, 11tc, 19cr; Zefa/Tony Craddock 96-7; Wendy Wrangham 118tl.

EL GEZIRA HOTEL: 131tr.

FOUR SEASONS HOTEL CAIRO AT THE NILE PLAZA: 60cl.

GETTY IMAGES: AFP/Cris Bouroncle 63br; AFP/Khaled Desouki 62tr; Bridgeman Art Library 10cla, 12c, 35c, 37bl, 41r; DEA/G. Dagloi Orti 7ca, 50-1, 102tl; DEA/S. Vannini 25bc, 25tl, 36cla, 36tr; Hulton Archive/ Keystone 64tl; Iconica/Eric Meola 31tl; The Image Bank/Daryl Benson 20-1c; The Image Bank/ Frans Lemmens 12-3c; The Image Bank/Sylvain Grandadam 38br; National Geographic/David S. Boyer 30c; National Geographic/ Kenneth Garrett 24-5c; National Geographic/Robert W. Nicholson 40cla; Photographer's Choice/ Stephen Studd 30cla; Popperfoto/ Bentley Archive 65cla; Robert Harding World Imagery/Oliviero Olivieri 36tl; Stone/Stuart Westmorland 8cla; Taxi/Jochem D. Wijnands 16-7c; Time & Life Pictures 41bl; Time & Life Pictures/Thomas Hartwell 64bl.

HEBA LINENS: 76tl; HEMISPHERE IMAGES: Jean du Boisberranger 61br; HOTEL SHEHERAZADE: 130tl.

KEMPINSKI NILE HOTEL: 79tl, 124tc; THE KOBAL COLLECTION: 20th Century Fox 48tr; Columbia 48br; EMI 48tl.

LEONARDO MEDIABANK: 125tl, 128tc, 133tr.

NOMAD GALLERY: 76tr; NOUR ELNILCRUISES: 27cr, 133tl.

PRESS ASSOCIATION IMAGES: AP Photo 64tr.

ZFL PRCo: 61tl.

For further information see www.dkimages.com

Phrase Book

The Arabic given here is the Modern Standard Arabic. This varies from the language spoken on the street (Egyptian Colloquial Arabic), which is a dialect of the standard language. Nevertheless, if you speak clearly and slowly you should have no difficulty in being understood. Transliteration from Arabic script to the Roman alphabet is a difficult task. You will repeatedly come across contradictory spellings in Egypt. Here we have given a simple phonetic transcription. The characters in bold indicate stressed syllables.

In an Emergency

Help!	an-n**aj**dah**!**
Stop!	qeff!
I want to go to a doctor	or**ee**d al zehab lel tabeeb
I want to go to a pharmacist	or**ee**d al zehab lel saydaliya
Where is the nearest telephone?	ayn y**oo**gad aqrab telif**oo**n?
Where is the hospital?	ayn t**oo**gad al mostashfa?

Communication Essentials

Yes/No	n**a**am/laa
Thank you	sh**o**kran
You're welcome	tashar**a**fna
Please (asking for something)	min f**a**dlak
Please (offering)	taf**a**dal
Good morning	sab**aa**h al-kh**ay**r
Good afternoon	as-sal**aa**m al**ay**kum
Good evening	masa' al-khayr
Goodbye	m**a**a as-sal**aa**mah
Excuse me, please	min f**a**dlak, law sam**a**ht
today	al-y**a**wm
yesterday	al-ams
tomorrow	**gh**adan
this morning	h**a**za as-sab**aa**h
this afternoon	al-yawm b**a**ad az-z**ohr**
this evening	h**a**za al-mas**a'**
here	h**o**na
there	hon**aa**k
what?	maza?
when?	m**a**ta?
where?	ayn?

Useful Words and Phrases

I don't understand	la **af**ham
Do you speak English/French?	hal tatak**a**lam engl**ee**zee/far**a**nsee?
I don't know	la **aa**ref
Please speak more slowly	men **fad**lak **taha**dath bebote'
My name is…	**e**smee…
How do you do, pleased to meet you	kayf h**aa**lak, tashar**a**fna be-mearef**a**tak
How are you?	kayf h**aa**lak?
Sorry!	**aa**sef
God (Allah) willing	ensh**aa**llah
Can you help me, please?	min f**a**dlak, momken tosaa**e**dnee?
Can you tell me…?	men **fad**lak qol lee?
I would like….	or**ee**d…
Is there…here?	**yu**gad…hona?
Where can I get…?	ayn ajed…?
How much is it?	kam **tha**man haza (m) **ha**zeehee (f)
What time is it?	as-s**aa**h kam
I must go now	labod an azhab al-a'n
Do you take credit cards?	hal t**a**qbal Visa, Access?
Where is the toilet?	ayn ajed al-ha**mam**?
Go away! (for children only)	**e**mshee!
Excellent!	momt**aa**z!
left	yas**aa**r
right	yam**ee**n
up	fawq
down	**a**sfal

Travel

driver's licence	r**o**khsat qiyaadah
I've lost my way	**a**na dal**ayt** at-tareeq
I want to go to…	or**ee**d al zehab le…
garage (for repairs)	gar**aa**j meekaan**ee**kee
petrol/gas	banz**ee**n
petrol/gas station	mahattat banzeen
A ticket to…please	law samaht, tazk**a**rat zeh**aa**b le…
airport	mataar
ticket	tazkarah
passport	jawaaz safar
visa	veeza
airport shuttle	baas al-mat**aa**r
When do we arrive in…?	mata nasel ela…?
When is the next train to…?	mata yaq**oo**m al-qet**aa**r alzaheb le…?
What station is this?	haz**e**he ay mahattah?
train	qet**aa**r
sleeping car	**a**rabat nawm
bus	otob**ee**s
bus station	mahatet el-otob**ee**s
boat	m**a**rkeb
cruise	j**a**wlah bahar**ee**yah
ferry	ab**aa**rah
taxi	t**aa**ksee

Staying in a Hotel

Have you got any vacancies?	hal y**oo**gad ghoraf khaal**ee**yah?
I have a reservation	**a**ndee hajz
I'd like a room with a bathroom	or**ee**d gh**o**rfah be-hammam
hotel	f**o**ndoq
air-conditioning	taky**ee**f
double room	gh**o**rfa mozdawajah
single room	ghorfa be-sar**ee**r w**aa**hed
shower	dosh
toilet	towaal**ee**t
toilet paper	w**a**raq towal**ee**t
key	meft**aa**h
lift/elevator	**mesad**
breakfast	fo**oo**r
restaurant	m**a**tam
bill	faat**oo**rah

Shopping

I'd like…	or**ee**d…
Do you have…?	hal **a**ndak…?
How much is this?	be-k**a**m haza?
I'll give you…	ha aat**ee**k…
Where do I pay?	ayn adf**a**a?
to buy	yasht**a**ree
to go shopping	yatas**a**wwaq

When two different vowels occur together, for example ae- and aa-, each is pronounced separately.

Sightseeing

mosque	j**aa**mea
street, road	sh**aa**rea
house	bayt
square	midan
beach	sh**aa**tee'
museum	m**a**thaf
church	kan**ee**sah
castle, palace	qasr

Eating Out

A table for…one/two, please	ma'**ed**a le-shakhs w**a**hed/le-shakhsayn, law samaht
I'd like…	or**ee**d…
May we have the bill please?	momken al-hes**aa**b, law sam**a**ht?
Enjoy your meal	bel-han**aa'** wash-shefaa'
beer	b**ee**rah
bottle	zoj**aa**jah
cake	kayk
coffee	q**a**hwah
– no sugar	– s**aa**dah
– medium	– mazb**oo**t
– sweet	– s**u**kkar zey**aa**dah
– with milk	– bel-hal**ee**b
cup	fenj**aa**n
glass	koob
plate	t**a**baq
sandwich	s**a**ndwetsh
snack	w**a**jbah khaf**ee**fah
sugar	s**u**kkar
table	ma'**ed**a
tea	shaay
mint	nean**a**a
(mineral) water	miy**aa**h (maadan**ee**yah)
wine	nab**ee**z

Menu Decoder

sh**o**rbah	soup
s**a**mak	fish
sal**aa**tat baazenj**aa**n	aubergine salad
s**a**mak sayaad**ee**yah	fish with rice
s**a**mak med**a**khan	smoked fish
sal**aa**tat baazenj**aa**n	aubergine salad
shamm**aa**m	melon
mekhallal**aa**t	pickles
h**o**mmos	hummus
zayt**oo**n	olives
w**a**raq a**e**nab m**a**hsee	stuffed vine leaves
b**aa**ba ghan**oo**j	aubergine and tahina paté
j**e**bnah	cheese
l**a**bnah	curd cheese
b**a**ydah	egg
shear**ee**yah	noodles
jamb**a**ree	shrimp
hab**aa**r	squid
t**oo**nah	tuna
lahm b**a**qaree	beef
fir**aa**kh	chicken
k**o**ftat daj**aa**j	chicken pieces
batt	duck
lahm d**aa**nee	lamb
lahm	meat
k**o**ftah	meatballs
luh**oo**m mashw**ee**yah	mixed grill meats
hamaam	pigeon
shaawerma	sliced split-roast lamb
boft**ay**k	steak
luh**oo**m mashw**ee**yah	mixed grilled meats
baazenj**aa**n	aubergine
abook**aa**do	avocado
kor**o**nb	cabbage
kar**a**fs	celery
felfel h**aa**mee	chilies
khiy**aa**r	cucumber
adas	lentils
khass	lettuce
b**aa**myah	okra
basal	onions
bat**aa**tes	potatoes
rozz	rice
tam**aa**tem	tomatoes
khod**aa**r	vegetables
mooz	bananas
faw**aa**keh moj**a**ffafah	dreid fruits
teen	figs
faw**aa**keh	fruits
aays kreem	ice cream
zab**aa**dee	yoghurt
bat**ee**kh	watermelon
baskoow**ee**t	biscuits
halawiy**aa**t	dessert
met**a**bbel	spiced
m**a**shwee	grilled
m**a**qlee	fried

Numbers

0	sefr
1	w**aa**hed
2	ethn**ay**n
3	thal**aa**thah
4	arb**a**ah
5	kh**a**msah
6	s**e**ttah
7	s**a**bah
8	tham**aa**neeyah
9	t**e**sah
10	**a**sharah
11	hed**aa**sh
12	etn**aa**sh
13	thalaath**aa**sh
14	arbaat**aa**sh
15	khamast**aa**sh
16	sett**aa**sh
17	sabaat**aa**sh
18	thamaant**aa**sh
19	tesat**aa**sh
20	aeshr**ee**n
30	thalaath**ee**n
40	arbaa**ee**n
50	khams**ee**n
60	sett**ee**n
70	saba**ee**n
80	thamaan**ee**n
90	tesa**ee**n
100	me**'**ah
500	khamsme**'**ah
1,000	alf

Days of the Week

Monday	yawm al-ethnayn
Tuesday	yawm ath-tholatha'
Wednesday	yawm al-arbe**a**a'
Thursday	yawm al-kham**ee**s
Friday	yawm al-j**o**mah
Saturday	yawm as-s**a**bt
Sunday	yawm al-**a**had

9/13

Selected Street and Regional Index

2x 1/19 (2/19)